Funny Face

Funny Face

PEGGI ◆ DAVIS

Archway Publishing books may be ordered through booksellers or by contacting:

Archway Publishing
1663 Liberty Drive
Bloomington, IN 47403
www.archwaypublishing.com
844-669-3957

ISBN: 978-1-6657-0555-4 (sc)
ISBN: 978-1-6657-0554-7 (hc)
ISBN: 978-1-6657-0556-1 (e)

Library of Congress Control Number: 2021907216

Print information available on the last page.

Archway Publishing rev. date: 05/21/2021

With sincere gratitude to
all of you who have encouraged,
mentored, and loved me.

Contents

Preface

All my life, I have been a chameleon; changing colors and honing hues to fit into new cultures and crowds. This painfully shy and awkward child became an amazingly adaptable adult and a lover of change. Whether it was partners, perceptions or places, my automatic ability to reset and reinvent has inspired my imagination, insight, and ingenuity. It has been a phenomenal yet peculiar journey. But with age come forgiveness and acceptance, along with a self-awareness I never knew. Finally, I can see it all clearly.

In her book *Pentimento*, Lillian Hellman wrote of the title's meaning: a departure, an artist's decision to change course. Although painted over, sometimes it is possible to see what was once there. That is my sojourn here. Like gazing through tracing paper, I am retracing my steps and incorporating my insights on my past and also our present. Sometimes with hesitancy, most often with humor. And always with hope.

“She’s making that funny face again.”

1

Funny Face

Saturday had finally come.

It wasn't just any Saturday. My sister and I were going to Radio City Music Hall to see a movie my mother had been talking about for months, based on the life of her model pal Suzy Parker. I think she was more excited than me, but she said I would love it. It was called *Funny Face*. That's what my daddy called me because I was not pretty like my sister. "She's making that funny face again," he said when I smiled with my mouth clamped closed for school and family photographs. But it was really because I was so self-conscious about my crooked teeth.

We were dressed in the baby-blue Viyella dresses that we'd saved for special occasions. Our crested cardigans smelled of Woolite, and our black Mary Janes shone like matching mirrors. It was chilly, and we were wearing our winter wool coats with the matching navy mittens. My mother was wearing her caramel-colored camel coat with the lovely lynx collar.

She was so beautiful.

After a bumpy bus ride, we arrived at the theater and bought our tickets. We sat in the center front row of the first balcony. The *tick, tick, ticking* newsreel came on with scary stories of a bloody battle in Cuba. Then came a sickening story about racism in a place called Arkansas. Next was a story about the USSR testing nuclear bombs. I wanted them to get the hell off the screen and let the movie begin.

Finally it did.

I saw the back of a gangly girl on a high ladder slowly shelving books. When she turned toward the camera, her face filled the entire screen. I gasped. I felt as if the *Encyclopedia Britannica* was laid on my chest. She had the most beautiful face I had ever seen. My mommy said her name was Audrey Hepburn.

The movie was about a simple shop girl who was discovered and became a famous fashion model. She traveled all over the world with lots of people taking her picture. There was a photographer, a hairstylist, a makeup artist, and someone called an art director. The art director checked that all the clothes and models were perfection and that the photographs looked like what she had imagined. She wildly waved her arms and whispered to the photographer as he worked.

Then photographs of Audrey flashed before my enraptured eyes. She was wearing the most outrageous outfits: fuchsia feathers, billowing ballerina-hued ball gowns, fluffy fox furs. The art director was delirious, delighted, and dancing around with her clipboard shouting, "Think pink. It's the color of the season."

Think pink. Think pink. Think pink. I was mesmerized.

Then Audrey was tiptoeing through a bobbing blanket of startled gray pigeons by a fabulous fountain in Paris; and then Audrey was running down the stone steps at the Louvre holding a canopy of colored balloons. Later, Audrey, dressed in a tailored trench coat, was wistfully walking under a big black umbrella shining with silver drops of recent rain. At the magic moment, when the light was washing a golden glow across her face, the art director yelled, "Smile *now*!" and my whole world lit up. I decided then and there that I wanted to be that person. I wanted to be part of that magical world of fashion, photographs, and fun.

I came out of the movie forever changed.

I drew pictures of beautiful clothes in my notebooks at school. I spent Saturdays studying the *Butterick Pattern Book* at the fabric store, and I learned to sew. I ran to the newsstand every month and grabbed the first copy of *Seventeen* magazine and crushed over cover girl Colleen Corby. I cut pixie-like Audrey bangs on myself and all my dolls. I practiced smiling from every angle imaginable.

And I waited.

A decade later, destiny ran its course. After years of books, boyfriends, and braces, I was promoted to art director and asked to create a spring fashion campaign for an elegantly edited group of pastel dresses. After long nights of drawing fashion layouts, writing headlines, and rehearsing my speech, I was scheduled to present it to the management board. I was totally terrified, of course, at the thought of speaking in front of a crowd for the very first time. As I stood up, I felt a curious calm come over me. I turned toward the crowd, slightly tilted my head, and gave them my most amazing Audrey smile.

I proudly announced, "Ladies and gentleman, think pink, and you'll never be blue." As I presented my ideas for a series of advertisements and plans for an outdoor location shoot, I watched them lean toward me, casually commenting to each other and nonchalantly nodding in agreement. With each new ad, their approval became obvious. As I concluded my presentation, I heard a robust round of applause.

I was exhilarated. Excited. Euphoric.

I was that person.

And yes, I was tickled pink.

"Dressed to the nines,

off we'd go to 21."

2

Dinner at 21

He looked like a movie star.

My paternal grandfather was bigger than life. Armed with his Saville Row suits, Cuban cigars, and well-bred British accent, his entrance into a room demanded instant attention. Soaring over six feet, suave, and sophisticated, his international impression left an immense imprint on me. Divorced and distanced from my grandmother, the suddenly single stockbroker became a social success at the upper-class clubs and cafés of Manhattan.

He had traveled and lived all over the globe.

Prior to entering the United States via Ellis Island, as so many Jewish immigrants from bombed-out London had done, Grandfather owned a successful import-export business. This afforded him a life of luxury in Argentina and India as well as the UK. His stories were magical, and my sister and I hung on every word. A comical and cultivated conversationalist, he held court almost nightly at the Big Apple's elegant establishments like 21, the Stork Club, and the Four Seasons. And the best news was that when a young Hollywood starlet was not on his arm, my sister and I were invited to an evening out on the town.

Dressed to the nines, off we'd go to 21.

We delighted in the escargot and the tiny little forks and the steak tartare clustered under the little silver domed trays. We would shriek with glee as the waiter woefully waved the live lobsters, waiting for our wide-eyed approval. We'd order sweet, steaming soufflés for dessert and learn what utensil was warranted for each course. We placed bread on the left, water on the right, and our young selves in the center of Grandpa's attention. We learned how to place our knives and forks when we were done, signaling the server to swoop in and clear the table. And we'd smile sweetly at the table hoppers, who oohed and aahed over our dresses as they exchanged pleasantries with our handsome host.

And if we were at the Stork Club, inevitably we were invited to join the joviality at table 50 with the powerful Walter Winchell. You see, our grandfather escorted the youthful Hollywood wannabes around town and was such a media magnet, he was a regular in Mr. Winchell's fabulously famous gossip column.

Yes, our grandpa was grand indeed.

Hobnobbing with the rich and famous ultimately proved productive for him, as he met and married a handsome (as they say) heiress of German descent. She was lovely, and owned an ironworks in New Jersey, to which she traveled daily in her Silver Cloud Rolls. They lived in a properly posh townhome in Sutton Place but also owned a beautiful gray-shingled home on a private beach on the Jersey shore, where my sister and I would stay in the guesthouse, which was the size of our apartment.

Armed with swimsuits, shorts, and sneakers, we unexpectedly learned that only dresses were allowed in the Big House.

"Body oil," we were told, "will get on the furniture."

As luck would have it, we were immediately escorted to the nearest shops and left laden with Ladybug dresses, much to our delight. Ladybug dresses, as those of you in my generation know, were a schoolgirl's Chanel suit at that time—something way too extravagant for our household. I might add that gifts of our most cherished clothes were not uncommon, and I remember receiving packages posted from Paris containing dresses of the finest fabrics and fashion. I specifically remember two, probably because I was asked to model them in front of my first-grade class. One was a gorgeous gray organdy dress embellished with lace, and the other a full skirt sprinkled with tiny rhinestones. I thought they were wonderful and wore them on every occasion I could. Much to my couture chagrin, we were promptly moved to a small private school that next year, compliments, I am sure, of our generous grandparents. There we were required to wear cranberry corduroy jumpers and white blouses every day. Despite the dour dress code, my sister and I adored our new school, where we both flourished.

Years later we moved away from New York, and our visits with our grandfather dwindled down to nothing. I don't know if there had been a family feud, or why he suddenly scooted out of our lives. I do know that I missed him terribly, and the magic he brought to our little world.

In retrospect, he was our rainmaker.

Today, memories of Grandpa seem dreamlike. But as my mind begins to question the magic of my memories, I look at the shiny sterling silver cigarette box that graces my home and read the carefully carved inscription. It is from a woman, obviously East Indian from her long, foreign name, and dated 1926. In her message, she asks that he remember her. Inside the box, you will find a faded black-and-white photo with white deckled edges. It had been taken on the deck of a large ocean liner on a brilliantly bright day. Standing on deck is a gentleman, tall, tan, and thin. He is dressed in white pleated pants and a tennis sweater, an ascot loosely looped around his neck. His shoes are of well-kept, woven Italian leather. In his right hand is a cigar, and in his left, a drink, most likely single malt scotch. He is obviously having a cheerful conversation with someone out of the camera's view. He is relaxed, savoring the soothing salt air, and deep in delightful discussion. It is my grandfather, and this photograph always makes me smile.

It has crossed my mind that sometimes things we leave behind become our legacy. As years pass, memories fade, people pass through, and inherited objects become the only messengers of our existence. Objects are reminders of people we knew, places we've been, experiences we've had, whether good or bad. And, at the end of the day, as generations come, and generations go, objects are really all that's left. We take our memories with us. But some reminders may be nestled away in a shining silver box, engraved with a message of "remember me," as we take our place among the clouds.

At table 50.

"Shimmering silver Christmas trees lined the lobby, emoting an elegant entrance to a fairy land decorated with dozens of diamonds."

3

The Golden Girl

It was an affair to remember.

I was euphoric; newly promoted at twenty-seven years of age to the management board of the city's hippest department store, after creating a series of advertising sections in the morning newspaper that were the talk of the town. My talent was that of ideas; creative ideas that saw sales surge. It was a dream come true. And to complete the picture of this Golden Girl's world was my new home and new husband. Gorgeous, and glib, he provided the yin to my yang, as opposites seem to attract. Our entrance together into a room was audibly noticed by the silence that followed.

We seemed to have everything.

My promotion was a surprise. And although I was grateful for the new opportunity, and the accompanying pay raise, I was most grateful to be included on the invitation list for the Corporate Christmas Party. Now an A-lister, with my handsome husband I would see and be seen. We would charm our dinner companions with titillating table talk and softly smile when hearing the workplace wives whisper, "Who's that?"

And then there's the dress. Of course, he would be dashing in his tuxedo, and I would wear a beautiful, black slip dress, made of the softest silk. It was weeks away, and my anticipation accelerated as the days went by. I was the envy of my peers. He thought nothing of it. Another boring evening with my work friends; friends with whom he had nothing in common, certainly not their baffling love of working twelve-hour days. Being in an office would make him cringe. No, corporate life was not for him. He was a free spirit, a man of his own making.

I waited.

The day came. Store scuttlebutt said the party, booked at a downtown hotel, would be fabulous. The retail group would occupy the main ballroom on the property's mezzanine, a floor dedicated to meeting rooms. Of course, around Christmas, there were several other parties being held that same evening. As we valet parked our new navy Fiat, I combed my hair and freshened my lipstick. He jumped out and rolled his eyes.

"Shoot me now," he mumbled.

As we walked in, the atmosphere was electric. Shimmering silver Christmas trees lined the lobby, evoking an elegant entrance to a land decorated with dozens of diamonds. The air smelled of cedar and cinnamon candles. Christmas carols played softly in the distance. People dressed in their holiday finest milled about, seeking directions to their appointed affair. The regal red carpeting led us to the grand staircase, the entrance to the festivities above.

We ascended.

As expected, there were several company parties in full swing filling the mezzanine. Ours happened to be in the first room. White tablecloths, tuxedoed men, crystal chandeliers; the room glowed with candlelight and purred with cocktail chatter.

I was in heaven.

The tables were numbered, and as we worked our way across the room, smiling and saying hello to all, we found our seats among the company's elite. Seated at our table were familiar faces from Finance, Merchandising and Human Resources. Our table was on the side, close to the paneled partition that separated us from a rather boisterous bunch next door, whose party seemed worlds away from the sophisticated dinner at hand. Small talk transpired; trends, sales, holiday plans. Wine flowed freely. By the time the main course was served, chatter ceased. The pleasantries had worn thin, and couples tended to murmur in each other's earnest ears.

Except for him.

The pounding in my head was only outdone by the pounding of the bass drum next door. *Boom, boom, boom.* The boisterous bunch were dancing, shouting, laughing. And then they were swaying, braying "Y-M-C-A," and the floor began to shake. I knew they were wildly flailing their arms in the air as they tried to keep up with the lyrics. They were plastered, sloshed, wasted.

They were insurance agents.

As our company chairman stepped up to the podium to elegantly express gratitude to his team, my sullen spouse excused himself and worked his way through the captivated crowd. As he slowly opened the ballroom doors, the music from next door grew louder. Now the party animals were doing the hustle. They were crazed, pumping their paunches and gyrating to songs from *Saturday Night Fever.* As the doors closed, the elegant party resumed as if someone had released the pause button. He had escaped. The restrooms were across the hall, adjacent to the raucous riot next door.

I waited.

Five minutes. Seven minutes, Ten minutes. The chairman concluded to thunderous applause that almost concealed the sound of the ballroom doors bursting open, slamming against their respective walls. Deafening music from next door began brazenly blaring into the silent soiree. And there, leading a conga line of twenty or so revelers, weaving their way through the candlelit tables of the openmouthed members of my management board, I saw *him*—bending, kicking, head thrown back in glee. Insurance agents laughing, singing, bunny hopping in a wild frenzy, as they hung on for dear life to their crocked colleague ahead. Finally, after multiple turns and twists, they circled back and bunny bounced their way out of the room, leaving my newfound associates aghast.

Of course, for me, it was the beginning of the end. It was never mentioned again, at work or at home. It was done. There was nothing to say, nothing to explain, nothing to do.

I waited.

Until late one night, after the dinner dishes were done, and the house was still, I danced into the moonlight alone. Endless possibilities filled my being as a million silver stars lit the way to the wondrous world awaiting me.

“It was sick-to-your-stomach stifling, and hotter than a steaming cup of café au lait.”

4

French Kiss

Searing, sweltering, New Orleans's decades-defunct French Hospital was my port into this world. It was July, eleven months after my resplendent, and later ravishing, red-haired sister was born. I remember seeing photos of my mom with us, sitting in the gentle green grass of Jackson Square park. She is cradling my sweet sister in her arms. I am the bump in her belly. We will be Irish twins and inseparable; in some ways alike, some ways different.

We did everything together, had our own little language when we were toddlers, and played with dolls way into junior high school. Overprotected and oblivious, we spent hours playing Parcheesi and Candy Land and cooking in our Easy Bake oven, discussing menus and meals that always ended up being the child-size cake mix we had on hand. I attribute my sister's and my ability to eat the same thing almost every day to this, although we live thousands of miles apart. We call it our "Psychic Food Network," and it constantly astounds my husband. Inevitably, when I ask what she is cooking for dinner, it is the same thing I have just popped into the oven.

We were Irish twins, literally, as our mother's family was a product of the Emerald Isle; our dad was born and raised in the UK. I think at this time my father worked at an astonishing antique store on Royal Street, only because years later we traveled from New York to New Orleans for the summer, while the owner went to Europe to shop. My dad, always armed with an ascot and a lovely London lexicon, managed the stunning store. It smelled of freshly polished furniture and was filled with inlaid antique armoires, magnificent mirrors, velvet chairs, carved carousel horses, enormous paintings with grand gilded frames, and a gleaming glass case of the most beautiful jewelry imaginable. In the 1980s I returned and purchased a set of child's gold matching French Cuff bracelets that I wear to this day. They are inscribed "To Little Emma, With Love From Father, 1853."

We tentatively moved into a one-bedroom walk-up apartment that summer, devoid of air conditioning, and a family of mice nesting in the worn-out sagging sofa. It was a far cry from our digs in New York. My sister and I shared the bedroom, and my parents slept on the rodent infested sleeper in the living room. Sparsely furnished and shabby to say the least. What I remember most was the unrelenting heat and oxygen-deprived days. It was sick-to-your-stomach stifling, and hotter than a steaming cup of *café au lait*.

I felt like I was on fire.

But the Quarter was colossally more colorful next to the New York City neighborhood where we actually grew up. Our summertime apartment was conveniently close to boisterous, booze-infested Bourbon Street. And because of its likely location, we had the awesome advantage of meeting and ultimately charming the Tiger Lady, who lived below us, and the Tassel Dancer, who lived above us. They were curious companions for us during the day, and we watched in awe as they applied their mounds of makeup in preparation for their exotic, erotic, evening performances. To us they were as enchanting as Elizabeth Taylor and glamorous to boot, and they pleasantly provided hours of amusing adventures for two nice but naive little girls. They spoke of their suitors as if characters in the family-forbidden *Peyton Place* and of the magic awaiting us with our first French kiss.

We were spellbound.

On the top floor, in the poor-man's penthouse, complete with a huge roof terrace, lived a lovely gay man who, for some reason, tended to us while my parents enjoyed an exciting evening on the town. There, the three of us would throw open the terrace doors and sing and dance to all the latest Broadway tunes under the starry sky. Much to the horror of the neighbors, I might add. I can still recall the lyrics to *My Fair Lady*, *Gigi*, and *The King and I* and the feeling of unabashed freedom as I twirled across the terrace. It was fantastic fun, and I loved stretching my arms toward the Southern sky and belting out "I Could Have Danced All Night" to anyone unfortunate enough to hear me.

I loved those evenings.

One evening, however, in the middle of another steamy sleep, I awoke to a man cutting through the screen of the window right above my bed. My screams, and then my mother's, scared him away. It is a memory from that summer that remains with me, and I am cautious to this day about open windows at night. For years, I slept on sweat-filled sheets rather than allow the evening breeze into my room. And then there were the night terrors that followed and my aversion to knives.

When the antique dealer returned from his journey overseas, we were invited to a delicious dinner at his fabulous townhouse, aptly appointed and complete with a beautiful brass elevator. It too smelled like freshly polished furniture and looked somewhat like his elegant store. It was a fitting end to our Big Easy encounter, but the leaves were turning, and school was starting, and my mom was eager to return to the only city she knew and loved. So off we went, back to our real life up north. Back to the lovely library with its stoic stone lions, to the splendid shows on Broadway, to our neighborhood gang with whom we spent almost every afternoon. Our young life there was creative, cultured, and classically 1950s.

New Orleans was an amazing adventure, and I returned dozens of times as an adult, drawn to the magical Quarter's cobblestone streets, fabulous French and Cajun food, and the soulful sounds of jazz that floated off the iconic iron balconies. That melancholy music would make me melt faster than a big bowl of praline ice cream. But nothing could ever replace the familiarity and freedom I felt on the spirited, stimulating streets of New York.

Nothing.

As the threads that tied our family together started slowly unraveling, and we left the Northeast for various cities and towns across the country, I learned to compartmentalize my feelings and developed an ability to change my focus like a red-beamed laser. It was a coping strategy that served me well and allowed me to adapt to the many changes to come. I was a chameleon, always watching and waiting for the other shoe to drop, ready to play the role expected of me. Always the new girl at school, I lived in my head until the bell rang at three, and my sister and I could be together again.

I couldn't imagine that this apprehensive, awkward girl would someday become a successful, somewhat sophisticated, sassy woman with a tribe of articulate and accomplished friends who were both creative and incredibly cool. Who knew that I would travel the world, have a captivating career, and then meet a dashing divorcé who would become my loving lifetime partner.

On a blind date, no less.

It was a charity event for St. Jude Children's Hospital, the joke being that he was the Saint of Hopeless Causes. And at forty-five, I was just that. But surprisingly, my date was handsome, intelligent, and an artist just like me, although he had changed careers to investment banking. He was a dream of a dancer, well traveled, and most importantly, ferociously funny. His wit was left of center, sharp as chicory.

It was a black-tie dinner, and as I peeked outside to get a glimpse of him, there appeared a gentleman gray at the temples with the most perfect pearly-white teeth I had ever seen. Whiter than the powdered sugar on my beloved beignets from Café Du Monde. His shoes were shined so fine, I could see his refined reflection from beneath his tailored tuxedo trousers as he sauntered up the sidewalk. It was love at first sight, and a split second of recognition that this was it for us both. We dined. We danced. We died laughing. He was captivating, charming, utterly and completely cool.

And he was hotter than a steaming cup of *café au lait*.

"It was a typical Texas panhandle
dust bowl of a town, with
absolutely nothing going on."

Welcome to Texas

I had a thing for Annie Oakley.

Totally taken with TV Westerns as a child, I had a decade-long dibs on being Annie whenever our neighborhood gang played cowboys and Indians. I had my handy holster and solid-red Stetson ready for a shoot-out at the drop of a hat. To be more believable, I had recently sheared the lovely locks off my Toni doll, braiding her hair first. I then attached them to the back of my ears, firmly fastened to the reddish-brown ringlets that brushed the back of my neck, with bobby pins pinched from my mom's stash.

I loved my braids and honestly thought, as children do, that everyone was fooled by my hideous handmade hair extensions. My massive mistake though was wearing them to our strict little school one day, and I was quickly discovered by the matronly, methodical Mrs. Conklin, our principal, who called my mother. This ended my fabulous future as a hairstylist/cowgirl/television star.

And then I discovered horses.

As a young girl, I loved the book *Black Beauty* like many of my generation. It was one of the first story books I remember my mother reading to us at bedtime, besides the horrific *Alice in Wonderland*, and that illustration of the oversized mushroom-induced Alice, with the long neck. My sister and I shrieked with fear whenever we saw it, and nightmares followed. And then, of course, there was Mister Ed, a talking television horse whom my dad thought was ferociously funny. I just never got it and hated having to sit there, concentrating on laughing at the right time, when his loose lips would curl and expose those huge buck teeth, just like mine. I thought he was creepy, like John Wayne Gacy with the clown face creepy. He sang this ridiculous song at the beginning of the show with his dumb, dismembered mouth. We were summoned to watch it with my dad whenever *Mister Ed* was on, along with that heinous Italian rodent puppet on *Ed Sullivan*, Topo Gigio. He creeped me out too.

I digress. Back to horses.

My first equine encounter was my make-believe horse Charlie, that lived at the base of our staircase to the attic. Armed with a curious cardboard saddle, stitched with purple yarn, I negotiated the stairs nightly to feed him and wish him sweet dreams. I don't know how long he lived with us, but I do know that most children had imaginary playmates. Not me.

Then we moved to a tiny town in Texas.

I am trying to temper my description of this place. The word *barren* comes to mind. It was a typical Texas panhandle dust bowl of a town, with absolutely nothing going on. Except a history of tornadoes. My parents promptly purchased a big barometer, and daddy dug a big hole under the house as our tornado shelter. To be honest, we were all petrified of them. Additionally, the landscape was flat as a flour tortilla. No hills; no valleys. No trees. The houses were cookie-cutter starter homes with flat front yards and a cement walk. Women wandered the neighborhood in housecoats and hair rollers. And the complete lack of zoning permitted a beauty shop housed in a tin trailer down the street. We were obviously seen as outsiders. My mom would dress for our revered riding lessons in her stylish starched shirtwaist dress and heels. City slickers, for sure.

I thought my mother was going to die.

There was a local celebrity called Honest Josh who gave riding lessons and somehow knew my father. Meeting a real-life cowboy was the most exciting thing about this entire town. After I was fitted with my prize black-and-white leather cowboy boots, my sister and I were signed up for horseback riding lessons. Now keep in mind, our only riding experience was the colorful carousel at Coney Island. But off we went, my sis on a medicated mare named Dolly, and me on a black stallion named, aptly, Thunder.

We went on Sundays, and learned the basics in the fenced corral, week after week. Then the day came for our first excursion on the trail. My sister didn't get far, as Dolly was determined to bite her, and kept nipping at her legs. Thunder, on the other hand, trotted happily away on the trail, much to my delight.

We rode and rode, and I eventually relaxed and let him lead the way. That proved an erroneous decision when Thunder decided he had had enough and turned and trotted toward the barn.

I concentrated on posting.

Then he began to canter. I held tightly to the reins.

And he began to gallop. I started to scream.

Soon, my feet, adorned in my adorable black-and-white boots, came out of the stirrups. Somewhere along the way I lost the reins. I was holding on for dear life. Everyone at the barn, including my hysterical mother, was screaming, "Don't jump, don't jump, don't jump!"

Clearly, that was the last thing on my mind.

Eventually we made it to the barn and I slowly slipped out of the saddle. That was the last time we ever saw Honest Josh. My horse fetish quickly turned to carefully collecting tiny china figurines that galloped along the top of my dresser. More my speed. Years later, I discovered Shetland ponies and had many splendid Saturdays riding them all over another town, galloping bareback, no less. It was the highlight of my week as a somewhat shy teen. However, horses have continued to influence my life in many subtler ways.

I learned to dance the pony.

I adore the Rolling Stones' song "Wild Horses."

I still wear cowboy boots.

So our nine months dealing with the dreadful drought of a town was not a total loss. Any experience, no matter how small, has an impact of some kind on our lives. It's amazing the things we take with us on our journey. Things that seem so insignificant at the time can mold or haunt us for decades. To this day, I have nightmares of tornadoes. I am always surrounded by them but wake up before the real disaster hits.

They say it means anxiety. No surprise there.

Not my childhood.

"Living in that town was a lifelong lesson that things are not always what they seem."

6

Mississippi Burning

We were aliens. Creatures from another land.

As new girls entering the local junior high, who had never seen or heard of a football game, or a cheerleader, or a pep squad (or a majorette, for that matter), we had trouble fitting in. Moving from New York to the Texas panhandle for under a year, we now called a sleepy Southern town our new home.

That became a whole other story.

To begin with, we couldn't understand what anyone said. Our little redheaded neighbor kept referring to her brother as Bubba, which confused us for months. And the girls in our class wore makeup and nail polish and had their hair done at the local beauty-parlor. We didn't even shave our legs. And to make it all worse, we discovered that girls our age were tormented into a public caste system with junior high sororities, with pins, parties, and parental legacies that insured their inclusion. It was a young girl's coming-of-age nightmare.

Lucky for me, there was another transplant from New Jersey, whose father was an officer at the local navy base. Quite the rebel, she was a perfect partner for my pliable personality. We terrorized the town in her 1957 Thunderbird convertible and amazingly were never caught at our antics. She too was perplexed by these social clubs because the girls took them so seriously. During their hazing phase, the pledges were on call for gifts of a member's desired desserts. We soon realized that with one mysterious phone call, with instructions on where to leave the poor pledge's prepared package, we were supplied with brownies and cakes and cookies or whatever our young Yankee hearts desired. We would pick them up, roaring with laughter, and then zoom down the street as fast as we could go, stuffing our cheeks with the fresh-baked bounty. Ultimately we assimilated into our classes and became friends with the girls our age.

Of course, we never complimented their baking skills.

Life in the South was so incredibly different. Instead of riding mass transit to the downtown library on Saturdays, we took tennis lessons and swimming lessons, and rode Shetland ponies all over town. We wore bras, and learned to wear Tangee lipstick and a touch of loose powder. We learned to do the bop and the limbo, and had Coke parties in our screened in porch. We were invited to countless slumber parties, a phenomenon unheard of up north.

Those slumber parties proved to be a rude awakening for me. It was common practice to stroll the silent streets at night as a group, and at these parties, it was part of the evening's entertainment. And as we rounded corners of upscale, white-bread neighborhoods, we would see huge wooden crosses brightly burning in some of the front yards. I had no idea what it meant, but I do know nobody took notice of it but me and my sister. It was life as usual for these girls, and the wild, whipping flames were no competition for the peals of laughter and long, lanky legs walking past these searing symbols of raging racism.

Our parents had a much harder time of it.

Once we were settled in a lovely little cottage with a huge, wooded front yard, we were fortunate to have employed a housekeeper. She was a lovely African American woman, and she and my mom became fast friends. One day, as they were having lunch at the kitchen table, the ladies from the church came for an unannounced visit. What was supposed to be a "welcome to the church" visit turned into a "you should never eat with the help" visit and ended with my mom throwing the women out of our house. She was appalled, and from then on, she rarely went to church with us, and we had to ride with a neighbor.

And then came the town's centennial celebration.

My dad managed a retail store downtown on Main Street. And after joining the Rotary as good businessmen do, he ended up volunteering to organize and manage the city's colorful centennial parade, the highlight of the week of historical events. The day finally came, and we were antsy with anticipation as we dressed for the big event. After a short ride downtown, we stood in front of my dad's store, preening with pride as the high school band began marching up the newly swept street.

The crowd roared.

Next came the floats, all covered in colorful crepe paper flowers, topped with beauty queens from the local junior college.

Then the mayor and the city councilmen, waving wildly to the spirited spectators. Followed by marching majorettes and banners and clowns and the celebrated Centennial Queen and her wide-smiled court, dressed in enchanting evening gowns with billowing skirts colored like the palest painted Easter eggs. *Oh*, I thought to myself, *to someday be a Centennial Queen!*

The crowd roared.

On and on it came. It was the biggest and best parade the city had ever seen. And as it continued to pass us and please us, we were caught up in the crowd's ardent appreciation for what my dad had done. Toward the end, the spirited African American high school band marched and swayed and stepped snappily down the street. They were magnificent. We had never before seen such energy and joy. Last but not least came the beautiful horses, decked out in flowers and topped with festive female riders in Western wear, beaming and gleaming with rhinestones shining in the sunlight.

The crowd was silent.

After an awkward time passed, the crowd dispersed and went home. We left perplexed at the stoned silence following the sassy sounds of the last band and the elegantly embellished horses and riders that silently signaled the parade's end. Unsure of what we'd witnessed, we returned home and waited for Dad to come home for dinner and shed some light on the subject. The exasperated explanation shocked us all. Late that afternoon, pickets began strolling in front of my dad's store with handwritten signs insinuating that my father was sympathetic to the town's African American community and not to shop in his store.

You see, the African American bands and dignitaries had always followed the horses. And you can imagine the problem it caused as they were forced to step in, or around, the massive droppings left by the anxious animals. It was the town's way of supporting the Southern Jim Crow mentality and keeping people "in their place."

We were horrified.

So despite the idyllic appearance of our sleepy, Southern town, racism was alive and well. I remember the Freedom Riders were planning to come through our city and the route was highly publicized. The public school system actually let the boys out of school to meet the bus armed with knives and chains. Hatred of the black community was generational. We just didn't belong. Eventually my father was promoted, and he was assigned to a larger store in a much larger city out west. My mother was ecstatic. The three of us stayed behind waiting for the school term to end and the house to be packed up for our new adventure. But the separation proved to be a strain on their marriage and a dark shadow slowly covered our pretty little home with the large front yard. Little did we know it would come in the form of a ghost.

We were all in a deep sleep.

I remember hearing my mother scream. It was a quick scream, almost a shriek, over as soon as it started. But loud, full of fear. Afraid to move, I lay stone-still in my bed before I worked up the nerve to creep down the hallway to her bedroom door. As I slowly opened it, I saw my mom sitting up on the side of her bed. She had switched on the little lamp on her bedside table.

"It's all right; go back to bed."

Relieved, I did just that, and the next morning nothing was mentioned about what I guessed was a nightmare. The week was no less or more than ordinary until that weekend. The Sunday newspaper had been delivered, and my mom was having a coffee while she read the paper, a ritual she did every week. Suddenly she gasped. Her hand flew to her mouth. I froze in fear. She turned white as a ghost, and I was afraid she was going to faint.

"Mommy, what's wrong?"

She showed me a photograph buried in the corner of an inside newspaper page. It was of a gentleman about my mother's age. He was tall and thin, and staring intently into the lens. He was standing against a weathered wooden wall and his dark straight hair was askew. "This man was standing by my bed the other night. It was why I screamed," she whispered. "When I tried to push him away, he just disappeared." Under the picture was his name, something unfamiliar to me. Also under his picture was a headline that read, "Former Resident Commits Suicide." The article continued to talk about his long life in our town, but that he relocated several years ago to another town about two hundred miles away. It said he was missed at his job, and days later the police had found him hanging from a rod in his bedroom closet. It gave his former address.

It was our address.

Living in that town was a lifelong lesson that things are not always what they seem. From the burning crosses to the breakfast in bed on a silver tray I enjoyed when sleeping over at my best friend's house, the social and economic suppression of the city's black community was hard to wrap my head around. And although we ultimately were included in the crowd that wore their sorority pins with preening preteen pride, the idea that young, insecure girls had to endure the social separation and rejection from them just seemed wrong.

But oddly, I relocated and retired in the South.

The race riots of the 1960s have passed, and yet I am constantly reminded of the cruel crevices they left in our community. My city saw many heinous acts of violence, and we are reminded downtown with historical signage and museums filled with photos and artifacts from our horrible, inhumane history. The city's crime has titled us as having one of the highest murder rates in the country. It is concentrated in the black community where pistols, pills, pain, and poverty reign. And yet it has grown better—much better, in fact—but not what it should be. City and state officials are diverse, as are many professions and universities. It is not unusual to see mixed-race couples and their stunning skinned children. People are more accepting and willing to help those less fortunate. This includes the vast homeless population that wander the streets, many mentally unstable and unable to care for themselves.

My heart bleeds for them.

The city itself flourishes in a setting of splendid scenery, world class restaurants, majestic mountains and streams of sunlight. Its beauty is breathtaking. Parks are filled with designer dogs and people of all ages walking or running in the crisp morning air. Children call their elders "Miss" while passing adults tell you to "Have a blessed day." It is friendly, genteel, and gracious. Cars stop for pedestrians, and church bells ring on Sunday. People deliver cream-of-anything soup casseroles for any bad turn of events, and Southern cooking is beyond compare. Doors are opened for ladies, senior citizens, and the disabled. It is almost idyllic.

And I love it here.

I don't know if old age has made me tired and accepting, but I do the best I can. I am kind and generous, and not judgmental. I know I can't change the world, but I do know I can tend the garden I've been given. So with that in mind, I live the Golden Rule and am forever grateful for my amazing abundance. And I give what I can to those less fortunate. I am not really a Southern belle and no longer considered a Yankee. I've been a Texan and a San Francisco flower child. I've worked in New York, DC and Tennessee. I am a made of a magical mixture of experiences from all over this wonderful country. The places I've been, the people I've met. And I am who I am.

An alien? Not anymore.

I am me.

"I need to see the suffering. I need to see the death. Because for me, seeing is believing."

The End of Innocence

We are speeding and afraid we'll be late.

I am with a group of happy, high school girls singing The Chiffons' latest hit, "One Fine Day," at the top of our lungs. We have recently moved again to another Texas town, but this one is a real city. The super-sized sky is colored a brazenly brilliant blue, and the air is electrically charged with excitement. The windows are down, bending our Aqua Net hair away from our fresh, full-of-hope faces. It is 1963, and we are on our way downtown to greet our handsome, young president and his eloquent, elegant wife, Jackie.

As we coast down Main Street, a car full of classmates pull up beside us, windows down, arms wildly waving in the air. "He's dead!" they yell.

That's the moment time stood still. For a week, we all sat at home, staring at our clothes washer–sized television sets in a zombielike state of mind. I remember watching that skittish, riderless horse, black as night, *clack-clack-clacking* down Pennsylvania Avenue. I remember the precious little boy saluting his deceased daddy, and the profound pain and fear for our future in my heart. I could put the two together. I could process the pain.

Today I cannot.

Twenty years back, I am driving to work. It is another day too beautiful to describe. The sky is devoid of clouds and is so brilliantly, brazenly blue it looks photoshopped. My window is down, and I can feel a slight breeze blowing across my face and fashionably flatironed hair. I am buoyant, blissfully content with my life in DC. As I'm bounding down the road, breezing through a light, the sky turns black. Not regular black as if a sudden storm is brewing above, but billowing black, dark as India ink.

And then comes the smell of fuel.

Unconsciously, I turn on the radio, expecting news of a tanker crash on the Beltway. But no; it was a plane, and it had hit the Pentagon, a quarter of a mile away. At the office, I watched in horror with my terrified teammates as the fearless fortress burned, and then on television as the two tiny planes repeatedly ravaged the Twin Towers and all those within. I remember the smoke, the sirens, and sounds of the jumpers, something I cannot erase from my mind. I grieved for the city in which I was raised and worked. I grieved for the first responders, the thousands of tortured people who had simply gone to work on time, and their families. I grieved for my friends; I felt their pain.

Today I cannot.

It is 2020. As I lounge on my luxe leather sofa today, I feel as though my mind has been scrambled like the week-old eggs in my refrigerator. I feel as if I've been thrust into *The Hunger Games* with Katniss by my side or am playing a minor role in the latest HBO horror film, reciting rehearsed lines. I feel like a Spanish spectator, waiting for the burly, fire-breathing bull to charge out of his chute. I am told there is a worldwide pandemic. Something I cannot see.

People are dismayed, desperate, dying. There is a new strain of virus, called COVID-19, we cannot control or cure. Its vitriol is universal. It takes no prisoners. And yet, as I sit here typing away on my terrifically thin Apple laptop, I look out my shiny, sparkling windows onto a beautiful, bucolic park, budding with spring. I am watching my flat screen television as I type, with my handsome husband and pet doodle dog, Dylan. They are close by napping. I consciously love my surroundings and my life—while a man on the news is doing a death count. He's warning me of more deadly days to come. "Be prepared," he solemnly states. The death count has surpassed 9/11.

I feel nothing.

My friend told me it is called cognitive dissonance … when what you hear does not match what you see. I am ridiculously relieved it has a name, that I am not delusional or uselessly unfeeling for the plight of others. I am relieved that it doesn't brand me as unsympathetic or uncaring. That I am not another blonde or "covidiot." I just can't believe this is really happening.

I need to see the enemy. I need to see the suffering. I need to see the death. Because for me, seeing is believing.

Hopefully, God willing, I won't.

And so I mindfully mask up and slide on my latex gloves as I walk our dog. I have groceries delivered these days, a privilege I never before allowed. I negotiate new recipes, read books, make cards and gifts, and watch movies and the time go by. I wipe down surfaces before I retire at night. And being retired by day, my life has barely changed.

Sure, I'm not lunching and brunching and flying high, but I'm certainly far from being bored or batty or blanched with fear. And yet, every day, as the death count soars, I wonder when this surreal state of the union will sway my sanguine state of mind. I wonder when this invisible enemy, invading and infecting our air, will disappear like a puff of smoke, wafting away into nothingness. I wonder when I will be upset, unnerved, undone as I was the day our vital young president was assassinated. And yet, that tragedy reminds me too of being that weightless young girl, riding with her new classmates in a car, the breeze blowing her brown bouffant as she sweetly smiles and sings her favorite tune.

I can no longer remember feeling so carefree. Is it even possible, at my old age, after all I've seen and experienced? I like to think so. I have to hope so. Just maybe.

One fine day.

“I was their Pygmalion, and I
was to bring the Bailey’s.”

8

Luck of the Irish

Growing up on big city streets in the fifties, we little ones played from dawn till dark outside with kids from our neighborhood. They were simple games … cowboys and Indians, jump rope and balls, potsy and hide-and-seek. The only thing that enticed us in, as the fire flies began to signal the afternoon's end, was *The Mickey Mouse Club.* That was our special time to drool and dream of being the astonishing Annette or grab a glimpse of the Triple R Ranch heartthrobs, Spin and Marty. It was a time of innocence, invention. and imagination.

Half the games that occupied us daily were simply made up. Statue was one of my favorites, and throughout my life, it has served me well. You see, my ability to remain stoically still, ferociously focused on a place or person across the room, has provided me with hours of eccentric entertainment. I possess an effortless ability to hypnotize myself into a Deepak Chopra–like meditation zone which, I believe, in addition to Bailey's Irish Cream, saved my life.

We'll get to that last one in a minute.

Having a sister only eleven months older than myself, I was graciously granted a lifetime BFF. We were incurably inseparable, but very different in many ways. Being the youngest, I was full of mischief and took great glee in playing copycat until she would cry out for our mother to make me stop. Being able to freeze-frame myself at will, I would always win … never succumbing to blinking or swallowing or making any gesture, however small, that would declare her victorious at my always annoying antics. These small victories made me feel puffed up and powerful. She nervously chews her lip to this day.

I think I drove her crazy.

When we were adolescents, our dad managed fashion retail stores, complete with gleaming glass windows filled with the latest looks, worn by tall, thin, world-weary-looking mannequins, molded after one of our mom's NYC model friends, Suzy Parker. We grew up embarrassingly enamored with the whole scene and on Saturdays would become part of that wonderful world in our own weird way. Dressed in coordinating clothes, we would literally climb into the windows, prominently strike a pose, blasé and bored facial expressions intact, and stand there still as statues for entertainment.

I am sure people passing on the street thought we were crazy.

I have been very uncool most of my life. I didn't really drink until my thirties and realize now I would have been much more fun in college if I had. As a young advertising executive, I learned to slowly sip Bloody Marys at our constant Press Club lunches and leisurely drain my wineglass over a date night meal or a nearby parched plant. I rarely purchased liquor unless entertaining or as a hostess gift, which is what sent me, after work one evening, to a downtown liquor store.

I needed a bottle of Bailey's Irish Cream.

I was being endearingly educated by my impeccably dressed, socially sophisticated, adoringly amusing boss. I was invited to another delicious dinner and entertaining evening at his beautifully decorated apartment, along with another close colleague and the company's fashion director. Those two gentlemen introduced me to a world I had yet to discover … company-paid weeks at The Plaza, Fabergé eggs, couture clothes. I was their Pygmalion, and I was to bring the Bailey's.

As I parked in front of the somewhat seedy store, I grabbed my bag and immediately looked for my assigned purchase. There was a Bailey's display, I was told, in the back of the store, to which I immediately headed. The display included a life-sized man holding a glass of the much-desired drink. As I grabbed a big bottle of the luscious liquid, I heard shouting at the storefront, and then realized what I was seeing. A man, wildly waving a gun, was threatening the cashier and demanding the panicked patrons up front to get on the floor, behind the counter.

I froze.

I froze next to the Bailey's display, holding a bottle of Bailey's Irish Cream. I froze and never moved, never breathed, and never blinked as the raving robber scanned the store. I swear he looked right at me. I felt myself retreating into myself. My fingers buzzing, my ears ringing, my brain repeating the decades-old delivery of insistent instructions: *Don't move, don't breathe, don't blink.*

His attention turned back to the cashier.

As this mad maniac grabbed the cash, I heard the gun go off. As he ran for the door, he pointed the gun and shot the cashier, but luckily only hit the mortified man's arm. With that, he was gone. Nobody moved for several seconds. We were all in shock. Long story short, we all gave our statements to the police and eventually left the store, the cashier in an ambulance and I in my car, grasping my big bottle of Bailey's Irish Cream. I honestly don't remember paying for it.

An hour later, as I entered the fabulous foyer of my bosses' apartment, I handed him the Bailey's. As he kindly air-kissed both my cheeks and welcomed me inside, he sweetly smiled and took the burdensome bottle from my slightly shaking arms.

"This is a lifesaver," he said.

He had no idea.

"There on the floor were my mother's fuzzy blue slippers, her footprints still pressed into their soft Shearling insoles, as if she had stepped out of them only seconds before and climbed the stairway to heaven."

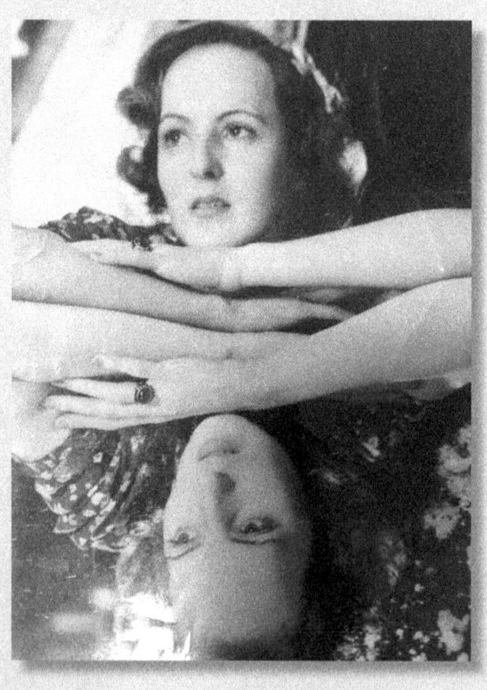

9

The Messenger

"Is this Peggi?"

A faintly familiar voice startled my twenty-four-year-old self out of my frenzied day at the office. It was my father, long gone after years of an unhappy marriage to my mom. They were still legally married, but he had chosen to begin again and had another family somewhere out west. My dad, an import from the UK, was quite lucky with the ladies. Short in stature but long on charm, he emphasized his origin by being a notoriously natty dresser and maintaining his "Downton Abbey" accent. It had scored him a voluptuous young bride, in addition to the older one, recently deceased. Of course, I didn't know this at the time. Our family was big on secrets.

And not just small ones.

"I'm cleaning out the house. If you want anything, come right away." My father's brisk British accent unleashed an abnormal burst of adrenaline into my system. He usually evoked no emotion in me, a self-protective apathy. I never felt a connection to him, as he was so emotionally distant even when he was with us.

A thousand thoughts ran rampant through my brain. What did I want? The diamond wedding ring that graced her long, slender hands? Her collection of Broadway show tunes? Her beautiful sweaters I was only allowed to wear for school pictures?

I raced to the little brick house I called home for the two years before my sister and I were sensibly sent away to college.

As I tentatively turned down our street, the rows of humble homes looked surreal. *Edward Scissorhands* instantly came to mind, along with a wistful wave of nostalgia. It was then I noticed a giant U-Haul truck behind the fins of my dad's long yellow Cadillac. *This should be interesting*, I thought.

I had no idea.

As I entered the living room with its tranquil pale gray walls and carpet, I realized my invitation was just another British formality. The room was vividly vacant, all packed up. The dining room was intact, the table covered with cookbooks, odds and ends, and accessories from throughout the house. The Capodimonte box from Italy, the antique Chinese iron daddy used as an ashtray when he smoked his pipe after dinner, the little French shot glasses I was told to grab in case of a fire.

Startled, I didn't know what to think or where to begin.

My dad entered the room from the kitchen door that led to the backyard. I noticed a girl, curiously close to my age, wandering in the grass. "Who is that?" I asked.

"A neighbor that came to help me," he answered. It was later that I noticed the "neighbor," actually his newest wife, was wearing my mom's diamond wedding ring.

My adrenaline surged.

And then a moment of clarity. The bracelet! The gold ID bracelet my mother had worn since she was a young girl. That was what I wanted. She would want me to have her cherished childhood gift from her decades-deceased brother. I headed toward the master bedroom. In the darkened hallway that ran the length of the little house, I was stopped in my tracks as I neared the bedroom door. There on the floor were my mother's fuzzy blue slippers, her footprints still pressed into their soft Shearling insoles, as if she had stepped out of them only seconds before and climbed the stairway to heaven.

I felt her presence, an overwhelming sense that I had a monumental mission to complete and that she would lead the way. I opened her bedroom door and took in the calm, ghost gray walls and familiar floral fragrance. All that remained was the dresser and a huge moving carton full of trash. The box was waist high and at least six feet in length and filled with trash, magazines, old clothes, books, and papers. There were boxes too, which probably held albums of photos and memories from our past. I wish I had looked, as I have no photographs of my childhood or family today. I glanced at the dresser that always displayed her personal belongings; her savored bottles of Chanel No. 5 and L'Air du Temps perfume, as well as the royal blue silk jewelry box from China, with its lovely lime green silk lining. It was a gift from my godmother and my mom's very best friend. The jewelry box was gone.

But my mother was not.

Suddenly a power, unlike anything I have ever felt before, led me to the far left corner of the enormous box of trash. As I walked to the far side, I saw the familiar magazines, clothes, and discarded memories. As I stood on my tippy-toes at the far left corner, so I could reach all the way to the floor, I pulled the little gold bracelet from its depths. There in my hand was my mom's ID bracelet, and I knew at that moment that she was with me.

I was so stunned, my body felt like electricity was running rampant through my veins. I told myself to breathe. Collecting and composing myself, I headed toward the front of the house, thinking my mission was complete. I wanted out. Away. I wanted to say my goodbyes and go home to my little apartment and grieve. Not just for my sweet, stylish, sensitive mom but for the *Father Knows Best* family I never had. Ours was a home built on secrets; hopelessly housing an unwavering undercurrent that things were never exactly as they seemed.

It always felt unclear, untethered, unsafe. Our fractured family put the "you" in dysfunctional. But today, my mother's spirit—or the all-knowing Man Upstairs—was in control. My dad was stoically standing by the front door preparing to leave, his nubile "neighbor" safely secured out in the sunny yellow sedan. As I walked up the hall, that feeling of a powerful presence returned. I was hit with an uncanny, unbelievable knowledge of my surroundings. Something was amiss. My hands were literally tingling, my mind was telling me I had more to do.

I looked up. It was the opening to the attic.

After being questioned, my dad admitted he hadn't looked into the attic, knowing full well that nothing he valued would be stashed amid the child-crafted Christmas decorations, handmade Halloween costumes, and old traveling trunks. Knowing with a calm certainty, I pulled the rope cord that lowered the worn wooden ladder and heard the familiar creak as I pulled it toward the floor.

And I climbed.

There at the floor's edge were two large cans I had never seen. Their worn labels were barely legible in the dank darkness. I strained my eyes to understand their contents, and when I did, I gasped. Inside were the long-ago cremated remains of my mother's parents. My gracious, gentle, generous grandparents had never been buried in their final resting place. But here they were, in plain silver-toned aluminum cans labeled by the New York funeral home that chillingly commanded the corner of our childhood block. Memories flooded my brain. *Breathe*, I thought.

I descended.

"Just leave those up there," my dad quipped. "No one will ever find them."

Of course, I didn't. I packed them into the trunk of my car, where they stayed until many months later when my sister and I could afford to bury them close to our mom. I pressed the gold bracelet onto my weary, willowy wrist and drove away. Away to a life of my design. A life full of music and art and dance and books, and all the beautiful things this life has to offer.

A life full of friendships, newly formed family, and faraway places.

And forgiveness.

"It wouldn't be Thanksgiving without a little cut to the bone."

10

Molotov Cocktail, My Dear?

Pass the oxygen tank, please.

When most people think of Thanksgiving dinner, that famously familiar family Norman Rockwell painted could come to mind. Not to me and my sister after the death of our mother, and the surprise surrogate family that preposterously popped up soon after. My father, you see, had started a new life and a new family out west, unbeknownst to my mother and us. He was living two different lives, and neither seemed to focus on us. The shit hit the fan, as they say, when our mom died, and the family secrets started pouring out like a fractured fire hydrant on a scorching summer day. Our new stepmother, it seemed, was the same age as me, and proudly wearing my mom's diamond wedding ring.

And she wanted us to be one big, happy family.

Well-rehearsed in avoidance, my sister and I had narrowed our family visitations to twice a year, once during the summer for

Daddy's birthday and once at Thanksgiving. They were always awkward, to say the least, and predictably while passing the turkey or dressing, our dad would drop some horrific family secret that would take our breath away. It was so nerve-racking and inappropriate, it got to be a joke between us as we dreaded and drove to our holiday horror show. It wouldn't be Thanksgiving without a little cut to the bone.

Think *The Family Stone*. On steroids.

I might add at this point that the "family" was not just the four of us, but three additional alien children at the gruesome gathering as well. And, having been raised to be polite and respectful and never to make a scene, my sister and I sat patiently at the table, ate what we were served, and waited for the annual bombshell. Our dad had always been distant, a stranger really, so this unpleasant and unmindful event was not far from what we thought of as normal. He was trying, at least, to pull us into the fold, but heedless of the collateral damage of it all.

And so we waited.

There was so much unfinished business that it was much, much easier to ignore the enormous herd of elephants in the room. Trying to fill the silence, our youngest new half sister began talking about her recent birthday party and what a celebration it had been. She mentioned the date, and a signal went off in my head. I realized it was the same date as my first wedding. The one where my dad just didn't show up. He had been working out of town and was to drive in that afternoon for the ceremony and dinner afterward. But no, he didn't show, and this Thanksgiving I realized why. Our new stepmother, in an untimely and unbelievable event, went into labor that very same day, with their first child. Neither of whom we knew existed.

As the years went by, the grenades grew and grew.

One year, he wanted to show us photos of our British cousin's children. I was sitting across the tenuous table from my supper-satiated sister. It seemed the meal had lasted for days. She had first glance of the two little boys we had never met as my dad passed the Polaroids to his right. She slowly glanced and then quickly glanced again. Well, glance is not the right word here. She stared at the small shot of two little boys sitting on their front stoop as the blood drained from her face. What she initially thought were little black beanies, were actually yarmulkes pinned to their pint-sized pates. As she passed the photos to her sexy new stepmother, who was smiling like a Cheshire cat, she looked at me with eyes bigger than the turkey legs we just decimated and mouthed, "Oh my God, we're Jewish."

And then the nuke.

It's hard to remember at what point the mushroom cloud came, covering us both with a dusting of debilitating disbelief. We were feasting on the traditional Thanksgiving turkey when my dad casually commented, "I got a call today about little Helen." Not knowing who he was referring to, we both let it slide and did not respond. Our mother's name was Helen, which prompted a sideways glance between the two of us, but neither spoke. We had learned not to ask questions. A few minutes and a few mouthfuls later, he continued with, "I would have thought she had died by now."

OK, I had to ask.

Until that moment, we had thought, and had been told, that our baby sister had passed away at birth decades ago. Not so. Seems she was taken to the nuns on Staten Island due to being born with spina bifida, where she lived until she aged out at eighteen. At that point she was moved to a city group home in Brooklyn and was now in her early forties.

I know all of this now, not at this dramatically dour dinner, because Helen had renal failure soon after, and they needed a relative to pull the plug. She had been told her mother had died at birth, but knew she had two sisters and looked for us all her life. The woman who ran the Brooklyn home and I corresponded for years after she died, and I learned all about her challenging life. I also received photos of her at holiday gatherings at this woman's home. She looked just like my dad.

I needed to get out of there.

Anxiously awaiting a break in the conversation, I proceeded to leave my body. My head was spinning, but my face was poised in a pleasant, polite part-grin. It was my camera face, something I had developed years ago when I was either insanely bored or angry and needed to maintain control. It was totally unbiased and unemotional. My little compartmentalized cover-up.

Getting up to clear the table, my dad continued to entertain the happy and fabulously full family with his stories. Chatting on, he began to walk us out to the car, totally oblivious to the shock and awe happening within his two twenty-something devastated daughters. I glanced at my sister, and she looked like a deer in the headlights. She was half smiling too—a big giveaway that she too was shattered. We waved good bye to their three children. We petted the family dog on the head.

We finally made it to the car.

Nobody is all good or all bad. And as angry as I've been when he asked me to buy his young wife a car, or send his children to college, I have always given him a pass. He has never shown emotion, one way or another. He was stoic, agnostic, and callous. But he worked hard to support us and is a product of his upbringing: sent off to boarding school at a very young age; his adulthood full of upheaval and uncertainty, as his terrified family fled their large London home when Hitler began his attack on the UK. But through it all, the little girl in me remembers that he is still the one who inspired my artistic endeavors, drew funny faces on the hard-boiled eggs in the fridge, the one who held my hand as I walked reluctantly into the waves of the Atlantic Ocean, and the one who ran breathlessly down the sidewalks of New York until I finally found my balance on my new Huffy bike. He did the best he could.

I thanked him for the dinner, because I didn't know what to say. I welcomed his usual, half-hearted, sideways hug, because I didn't know what to do. I told him I loved him, because I didn't know how to feel.

Throughout the coming years, my dad would visit me in the cities in which I lived. He popped up in Texas with his then grown son. It was during that visit that I learned he had moved to Missouri with him and his new daughter-in-law. Evidently, he didn't like it. One night while they were sleeping, my dad crept out of their house with a few of his belongings and drove all the way back to Texas. It was from there that he decided to visit me again and rode the Greyhound bus all the way to San Francisco. Somehow, he landed in Oakland, where I got the call that he had arrived. He loved the city, but the hills proved too much for the weakness in his legs. Another call came at bedtime while I lived in Manhattan. It was the police telling me he was at the Lost and Found in Penn Station, and I needed to come get him. I grabbed a cab and found him sitting in a wheelchair gorging on cookies and Coca-Cola, chatting up the girls in the office.

I put him in a hotel around the corner from our flat.

Despite the lack of warning, we had a nice visit. He was happy to be back in New York, and though his cane was barely carrying his carcass, he was able to visit the neighborhood deli and go on cab rides to see all the city's changes. His hearing was waning too, so conversation was limited. But he seemed content to sit on my couch and watch television and tell me about how he met our mother and his travails in the United States. He got teary-eyed as he talked about little Helen.

The leaves in New York were starting to turn, and the air was crisp with the season's change. There wasn't a cloud in the sky. It could not have been more beautiful. One morning as I routinely walked him from the hotel to our brownstone flat down the sidewalk bowered in gold and rust foliage, I was overcome with a sense of peace and the thought that life always comes full circle. Yes, my dad was a character, a man who made his own rules and always followed his desires. He made a lot of missteps along the way, but he seemed to reconcile them in his own muddled mind. We walked slowly, stepping over the chestnuts and concrete cracks. We greeted doormen on the way and petted the neighborhood dogs out for their morning stroll. He leaned on me for support, my arm linked in his, and I knew this would be the last time I would see him. But it was such a perfect, placid, peaceful moment in time.

And the one I choose to remember.

"As I perused the map, I noticed a nightmarish notation on the reliable Rand McNally. It said, The Sagamore Bridge. Oh my God, a bridge."

11

Nantucket Nights

She said we had to see Nantucket.

Newly divorced and champing at the bit, my bestie announced this one Saturday evening as we watched *The First Wives Club* for the fifteenth time that we must see Nantucket. It was an offhanded comment, as we were totally immersed in the movie and knew most of the dialogue by heart. Years later, and who's counting, we and group of very close friends got so wasted one night that the three of us actually began singing "You Don't Own Me," using candles as microphones, lined up and marched out the front door, and paraded down the richly residential street singing it at the top of our lungs. And I have pictures.

But back to Nantucket.

It was amazing that we hadn't been there before, with the number of beach location shoots we had been on together—she a fashion photographer, and I an art director. We actually met on a job shooting photographs in a southwest city, a trip that defies description to this day. We were scheduled to photograph people and places that made the city great for a new department store opening. The list was long, but the days were longer, and we had endless problems at the time that later turned into our most hilarious stories.

The first morning we were to shoot a men's organization. Not knowing what it was, we were amazed to find about thirty past presidents of the well-known nonprofit group, all of whom must have been in their eighties or older, waiting at the assigned location. Unfortunately a few were running late. As we waited and waited, the free coffee being served led to a colossal caffeine overdose in the geriatric gentlemen, who were whipped into a frenzy. They were laughing and shouting and changing seats, totally unhinged. Walter wouldn't sit by Harry, George wanted to stand, Lyle wanted to go home, Leonard was about to sock poor Oscar in the nose. It was total chaos. We finally photographed them as best we could and got away unscathed.

Late that afternoon, we were to meet the mayor and his wife at their mountaintop home for a quick interview and a photo. Unfortunately, we beat them home, as they had attended a cocktail function beforehand. As they finally drove up the long gravel drive and exited their car, it was obvious that they both had been vastly overserved. Especially the wife, who resembled Flo on the TV show *Alice* and whose wig had been jostled to the left and was almost hysterically horizontal on her head. She could barely walk, much less talk, and innocently inquired who was going to do her hair and makeup. I immediately pointed at the photographer and said, "She is."

I thought she was going to kill me.

The week went downhill from there. But after a quick trip up the mountain to Santa Fe one beautiful evening under a blood-orange sky, the crew had a wonderful wine-infused dinner and a lovely, lazy ride back. The stars were bright and brilliant in the navy blue sky, and the air was as crisp as the marvelous Mexican tortillas we had just devoured with dinner. We spent the magical trip returning to the hotel singing Simon and Garfunkel songs to the radio as loud as we could and came back the very best of friends.

And now we were going to Nantucket.

We flew to Boston and rented a car for our journey. She was the driver; I was the navigator. After several loops around the Logan Airport parking lot, we eventually found the exit and headed toward Hyannis and a wonderful week of sand, shopping and seafood on Nantucket Island. I must inject here that I was not a great person in a car. My phobias of speed, getting lost, and bridges had escalated since my divorce. It has all declined but stays with me to this day. As I perused the map (this trip was in the eighties, pre-GPS) I noticed a nightmarish notation on the reliable Rand McNally. It said, "The Sagamore Bridge." Oh my God, a bridge. My stomach clenched in horror. As I eyeballed the encompassing distance, the dreaded Sagamore was less than an hour away. Mile after mile, my apprehension grew, and when it finally started to rain, I lost it. We just could not cross the savage Sagamore Bridge in the rain.

We agreed that if it was raining as we approached the menacing river's rapids, we would smartly stop for lunch. If it was dry, we would hold our breath and forge ahead. After several heinous hurdles around our first experience on roundabouts, I settled back down. Me screaming, "enter six o'clock and exit two," to keep us on the perilous path ahead.

We were ten minutes away from the beastly bridge.

I was nauseated with fear. The rain stopped, and three minutes away, we decided to go for it. We steeled ourselves to surge steadily ahead across the danger that awaited. We saw the scaffolding. We approached the sign. I held my breath, and onto the bridge we went. And then we howled in hysterical laughter.

The bridge was only two car lengths long.

The rest of our journey to the Hyannis ferry was less than memorable. But once we got to our idyllic island destination, that would soon change.

We met him at 21 Federal. Zagat said it was the restaurant you'd remember. Gorgeous, gregarious, and a glassblower, he lived and worked on the island. He offered champagne, then dinner, and then the same, night after night of our stay. He seemed mesmerized by us, Lord knows why, and thought nothing of meeting us every evening for our nightly entertainment and meal. We learned he had apprenticed with Dale Chihuly, a master glassblower whose works brighten the Bellagio's lobby in Las Vegas, among other famous installations. His uncle was a major film producer in Hollywood and his cousin a household name. He was interesting, intriguing, and intense. As our final night drew near, he suggested we add a gentleman friend of his to the mix, a Boston attorney, and go out for a celebratory dinner.

And so we did.

The chilled champagne flowed as we dined on the best Nantucket had to offer. Things were heating up between me and this mysterious artist, and he suggested we go see his home and studio. Off we went to the other side of the island, knowing full well we needed to pack and get back to Boston in the morning for our flight home. However, the champagne, with which we were massively overserved, clouded my muddled mind, and yes, I was defenseless with this gorgeous hunk of a man, while my friend spent the next several hours fighting off the tagalong attorney from Boston.

I thought she was going to kill me.

I started getting nervous after my desirable date fell sound asleep, knowing we had a flight to catch. I finally noticed that there was a clock radio across the room. The room was so dark, the blackest black ever, that all I could see was a brightly blasted 10:37. Thinking we had plenty of time, I nestled in to take a short nap. Upon awakening, I again checked the clock radio. 10:37 it said. Thinking I had just conked out for a minute, I snuggled back down and closed my eyes. Now remember, we were on an island with no streetlights. To say it was dark is an understatement. The kind of dark that keeps you from seeing your hand in front of your face. It was still 10:37. I got up and crawled to the clock, and much to my alcohol induced horror, realized that 10:37 was the radio station, not the time. Terrified, I knew I had to find my friend.

I started crawling, following the edges of the room, following the baseboards, looking for the door. At one point, I ended up in the closet, which must have been open, but couldn't seem to find the way out. It was getting light out, and I knew we were in trouble. I particularly knew *I* was in real trouble. I finally found the door and my furious friend, woke up the boys, and returned home from our infamous evening. As we threw our creased clothes into our suitcases, not a word was spoken.

Into the car and off we went, speeding toward the ferry at an alarming rate. We just made it. I was green and queasy beyond belief. Between the champagne, the frenzy to leave, and the choppy waters, it was all I could do not to get sick. It was the longest trip of my life.

I thought she was going to kill me.

Back into the car, screeching down the country roads, across the perilous Sagamore Bridge, through the touch-and-go Boston traffic, and into the rental car lot at Logan Airport, we had minutes to spare. It was a miracle we made it, but we still had not spoken. After checking our luggage, we ran to the gate and took our seats. We looked at each other, and all at once we started laughing, and howling, doubled over in hysterics. We couldn't look at each other without falling apart. I am sure people thought we were drunk.

Imagine that.

To this day, she says she has never been madder at me. But to this day, we still howl about it. Once home, I was greeted with ravishing red roses from my new Nantucket suitor. And after nightly talks on the telephone, I returned to Nantucket one weekend to see him. It just wasn't the same. They say vacation romances have a 7 percent chance of becoming long-term relationships. Not good odds. And research shows that the psychological stimulation of being in a new place can create strong initial romantic attraction. So the lines between romantic attraction and being physiologically stirred could easily be blurred on our travels.

Blurred is a good description. But I have built my life on experiences that give me stories to tell. Because in the end, you won't remember those meetings at the office or all the people you barely know who make up your list of Facebook friends. It's experiencing life that counts, wanting everything this world has to offer. Seeing everything you can. Doing everything you can. Mark Twain wrote, "Twenty years from now, you will be more disappointed by the things you didn't do than by the ones you did do." And he is right.

We knew we were having fun.

We just didn't realize we were making memories.

"For over half a century, a group of six creative, close colleagues have dressed and delivered Ho Cho Chuckie to almost every major event in our lives around the world."

The Gift from Gump's

It was the gift that kept on giving.

Wondrously wrapped in a seasonal signature Gump's box, it lay nestled among the generous gifts under the tree. It was labeled for my bestie, with whom I shared the holidays for years. Both successful, single, and sassy, we were inseparable for decades. We tried to guess the beautiful yet burdensome box's contents. A fabulous lead crystal vase, an ivory mah-jongg set, a shining sterling silver carafe? We just knew it was something awe inspiring, something too fabulous for words, and decided it was to be opened last.

The big moment came.

I held my breath as my friend lifted the heavy object of our desire, softly swaddled in tissue paper, out into the crisp Christmas morning air. Slowly unwrapping, we were mystified until it became apparent the gift was not shining silver, or crystal or antique ivory. It was made of solid wood, and appeared to be a hideously painted crouching Chinese pillow boy statue.

We were aghast.

As we cleaned up the Christmas chaos, the heinous statue sat under the tree like a threatening troll waiting to thwart our holiday cheer. We spent part of the day watching a horror movie about an evil puppet named Chuckie. That evening as we prepared to call it a night, my mischievous mind made me grab the statue and put it in the microwave, and wait for the startled scream the next morning.

It came.

Hiding the statue became a game. We named him Ho Cho Chuckie, and this unsightly statue took on a life of its own. For over half a century, a group of six creative, close colleagues have dressed and delivered Ho Cho Chuckie to almost every major event in our lives around the world. And each time, the game was upped. After photographing him wrapped in duct tape to a child's chair and demanding a ransom for his safe return, I actually received phone calls from brusque bondsmen at all hours of the night. Seems my phone number was published in a big city newspaper's personal column offering a large ransom for finding Ho Cho Chuckie.

He has appeared baked inside a birthday cake, topping an elegant centerpiece on a heavily flowered fruit display at a corporate function, brought in wrapped and beautifully veiled with orchids at my wedding in Hawaii, and found casually sitting at a bar, martini in hand, in a tailored navy blazer, at my sixtieth birthday party in Dallas. He was discovered dressed as The Scream on a Houston Halloween porch. He has been placed in the center of a lazy Susan at a Southern luncheon, hidden in a toilet, and as a stowaway passenger on a train traveling across China.

The latter was planned as his demise.

As the pressure to outdo each other increased, the time and expense of shipping Ho Cho (as his name later became) around the world had become extravagant. So as a trip across China became a reality, the group decided that leaving him there would be fitting as Ho Cho's final resting place. At one point, we boarded a timeworn train and decided that during the journey, Ho Cho would be tenderly tossed out the window, like a dove taking flight into eternity. As the big city skyline became smaller and smaller, we left him by the compartment's curtained window to await his flight into the captivating Chinese countryside. We decided to have lunch first in the oddly decorated dining car before the ceremony.

Our journey introduced us to a myriad of Chinese dishes, not available at our local Asian restaurants. It was a good thing, as they were unrecognizable and unsavory. Hundred-year-old eggs, clawlike chicken feet in the steaming tureen of soup placed before us every evening. Bowls of warm, wormlike meats, unlike anything we had ever seen. Everything was placed on a lazy Susan in the table's center. I remember it spinning endlessly as we all lunged for the rice bowl.

We lived on rice and Chinese beer, something I have never given up.

When we returned to our compartments, Ho Cho was gone. Our plan was foiled and another mystery begun. Would he appear again in China? Would he make it home to the States? That was thirty-five years ago, and the game continued.

And continued.

The last time I saw him was at my friend's sixtieth birthday luncheon at an upscale Dallas restaurant. I had arranged with her fiancé to include him at the festivities. Ho Cho had evolved at this point, now a timely trannie named Caitlin, dressed in shiny stone jewels and a golden gown, which matched her beautiful new turban topping her gloriously styled beach waves. She was the guest of honor.

We are all waiting to see Ho Cho's next incarnation. Time between sightings has become longer as we all live the last of our lives, with new husbands, houses, and health issues. Our friendships continue to this day, closely tied, bowed with ribbon, like a precious, perfect present.

We have weathered the best of ourselves and the worst of ourselves, across time and distance, for decades. And the magic provided by an unsightly pillow boy statue, many moons ago, is a testament to the power of ingenuity and inventiveness. But it is also a testament to the devotion and dedication of six crazy-assed lifelong friends making each other's worlds a little more lighthearted and loving. A wonderful world full of astounding anticipation and splendid surprises, not unlike a beautifully wrapped gift, under a little lighted tree, from a Christmas long ago.

"It's not an optical illusion.

It just looks like one."

13

Trompe l'Oeil

I grew up with a potato always sitting on our coffee table.

Not a real Idaho spud but a carefully carved brown rock with eyes, a true optical illusion. It was the result of my free-wheeling father's love of trompe l'oeil and whimsy. Something my sister and I share to this day. In French, *trompe l'oeil* literally translates to "deceive the eye." The artistic technique intends to make a painting or design appear to be a real object. And that's what that tater did.

Decades later, I was given a Tiffany ceramic plate that held three perfectly extraordinary eggs. I adored it and immediately placed it on my coffee table for years to come. My sister now has not only that pretentious potato but a ceramic plate scattered with lifelike chestnuts. It's amazing how insignificant incidents repeat themselves later in life. And how optical illusions play such a role in our lives. If we see it.

In 1967, the Summer of Love, the Beatles released their iconic album *Sgt. Pepper's Lonely Hearts Club Band.* A group of us stayed in our small college town for summer school and were all enrolled in one art class or another. My roommates' teacher was a friendly, rebellious young man who spent an enormous amount of time at our apartment, something we were too naive to question. We just thought he found us way cool. Anyway, his curriculum consisted of analyzing the lyrics to *Sgt. Pepper*, under the course name Sgt. Petter, which was our maiden name. Again, it just amused us, but later we learned his motivation. My man-magnet sister received an F in his class after refusing to sleep with him. My, how times have changed and the lessons learned. Ralph Waldo Emerson wrote, "There is an optical illusion about every person you meet."

I think this was my first lesson.

In *Sgt. Pepper*, there is actually a song about illusion called "Within You Without You." With its haunting Indian sitar sound, composer George Harrison wrote, "We were talking about the space between us all, and the people who hide themselves behind a wall of illusion." The message is clearly a hint of the oncoming counterculture. Harrison had recently traveled to India and was evolving away from the traditional Beatle beat. He also was responsible for including the yogis on the popular album cover. His message was clear: Not being our real selves is detrimental to all of us, as we are all one in the universe.

I have recently learned there are three main types of optical illusions, including literal illusions, physiological illusions, and cognitive illusions. All three types have one common thread. The image seen by the brain doesn't add up. That's why optical illusions are referred to as a "trick" of the eye. And the eyes, they say, are the mirror to our soul.

It's not an optical illusion. It just looks like one.

Once there was a seriously handsome man who was the Paul Newman of his work world. With baby blue eyes and a chiseled chin, he was responsible for the employees' career paths and well-being within the company. It was a fitting choice for someone so seemingly sympathetic and attuned to people's needs. He walked the walk and talked the talk. His self-deprecating sense of humor served him well, especially when he brazenly became the so-called suitor of several employees. But what people misunderstood was that he was an optical illusion. An insatiable romantic, old Blue-Eyes could lie to your face with such authenticity that it was like living in a smoke screen of seduction. A stained veil of disrespect. He looked so earnest, so empathetic, so endearing. It was a kinship of delusion that transformed into disillusion and dismay.

Too often.

Researchers tell us that there are different types of liars. Pathological liars show little regard for others and tend to be manipulative in other aspects of their life. They lie with such conviction that at times, pathological liars can actually believe the tales they tell. Compulsive liars have little control over their lying. They may be telling the same lies as the pathological liar, but their intent is different. Usually compulsive liars lie out of habit and just can't stop. It took many of old Blue-Eyes's corporate conquests way too long to catch on, something hard to watch. My mother taught us, "You can't judge a book by its cover." And she was right. But books aren't like people.

Books are safe.

I have a ferociously funny friend who one day decided that she had had enough of the Houston heat and the toll it took on her upstairs window boxes. So on a steamy Saturday, off we went to find a perfectly acceptable alternative. The problem with besties shopping together is that it is synergetic. What's good for one is great for both. We ended up at a local crafts store, and upon discovering that, after a wine-infused lunch, I might add, we could not tell the difference between a group of faux red geraniums and the real thing. We were elated and bought over fifty red silk blooms that day and happily headed home to plant.

The following weekend, my then-boyfriend, now my hilarious and handsome husband, flew in from Dallas, his first visit to my home. Of course, I wanted everything perfect for his inaugural visit—furniture polished, candles blazing, wine chilled, and my back deck ablaze in colorful crimson blooms. After a romantic and really late evening, we made our way to the master bedroom which overlooked the garden. A late riser, I woke to an empty bed. As I gathered myself from my 1980s multilayered Ralph Lauren bedding, I could smell the soothing scent of coffee in the air. As I threw on my robe, I noticed my new love wandering around on my divinely decorated deck below.

He was watering the geraniums.

Our friend Ralph Waldo Emerson, who warned us about optical illusions of the human race, also told us, "The earth laughs in flowers." The sight of my sweet, sincere suitor watering the faux flora outside did make me break into gleeful giggles. It was years before I ever told him. We laugh about it still. And to this day, every time I visit my beautiful, black-thumbed friend, and we pull into the driveway of her handsome home, I gaily gaze up and see two fabulous flower boxes ablaze with ravishing red geraniums. It's our little secret.

And her secret garden.

"It felt like flying, like Peter and Wendy happily hovering above the lighted, legendary London town from my storybooks of long ago."

14

And So I Dance

I have been asked all my life if I was a dancer.

I am assuming it was because of my small frame, not my expertise—although I have to admit I would kill to have been a ballerina. And it wasn't from lack of trying. Growing up in New York, mecca of the arts, I was lucky to have seen *The Nutcracker* at Christmas several times, performed by the awe-inspiring American Ballet Theatre. The music still takes me back, especially the "Dance of the Sugar Plum Fairy." It was there that my visceral vision of daringly dancing on pointe began. It's something I still dream about.

Of course, I took ballet as a child.

Recently, my British cousin came to visit in celebration of her seventieth birthday. We hadn't seen each other in over sixty years, so it was quite a homecoming, as she had lived with us for a year at the age of five. During that time, she attended ballet with me and my sister, something I really had forgotten. In her lithesome London lilt, we were actually reminded of our Wednesdays with Mrs. Goobler, dressed in pale pink tights and soft ballet shoes. Of course, I would have preferred pointe shoes but was way too young and incredibly inexperienced to have them.

And so I made my own.

I was curiously creative as a child. I made my own clothes—my doll clothes too—and drew catalogs of princess dresses and elaborately embellished shoes and accompanying accessories. I had an imaginary horse that lived on the landing to the attic and a myriad of childhood fantasies. One of them was dancing on pointe. Armed with two empty orange juice cans, pink paper, Lepage's glue, and mounds of confiscated cotton balls, I proceeded to stuff my poor little feet into my creation. After a few disasters that landed me flat on the floor, I mastered the searing pain and danced my way down the sidewalks of our neighborhood. Peerless posture, head up, arms beautifully bent, hands perfectly poised. Gelsey Kirkland had nothing on me.

And so I danced.

Thursdays at our little school included two hours of ballroom lessons, at which I excelled. I loved those classes and competitions, always winning the lindy and the waltz. I made my mother proud as I pranced around as if a spotlight was shining only on me and the tiny blazer-bound boy who was my partner. I had rhythm and was ruthlessly pliant and poised, limber and lithe. Gliding across the hardwood floor transported me to another realm.

It felt like flying, like Peter and Wendy happily hovering above the lighted, legendary London town from my storybooks of long ago.

And so I danced.

As I we moved to other cities, my bond with ballet waned and gave way to the teenage twist, high school hustle, and college with its cannabis-fueled cavorting. I loved spinning and swaying to Motown, losing myself to the long version of the Doors' "Light My Fire" and all the spectacular songs of the sixties. My happiest times were definitely dancing at fraternity parties for hours on end. A far cry from the graceful gestures of my beautiful ballet. But as I moved beyond my schooling, married young and began a career, I once again longed for that freedom of movement, that poignant patter of the piano that took me to another world in which there was nothing but the music and me.

I enrolled in adult ballet.

I continue to take adult classes as I find them, few and far between. I've learned the hard way that many classes labeled "beginner" can be anything but that. My last exasperating experience found me bumbling and fumbling across a studio floor like an oxygen-starved flounder. I never went back. So now my little pink shoes are nestled in my closet, again waiting patiently for their curtain call. In the meantime, I choose my cherished classical tunes and playfully pirouette around our house, until my spinning renders me dizzy. I *cabriole* and *changement* to my heart's content, *arabesque* and *attitude*. I know them all. My husband is adoringly amused and accepting of my need.

I am crazy.

He is my biggest fan.

Recently I read Michelle Obama's autobiography and was stunned by a passage describing Sasha's joy when playing a mouse in the magnificently staged Moscow Ballet's *Nutcracker* one Christmas Eve. She wrote, "But she was young enough still that she could give herself over to it, at least for the moment, allowing herself to move through this heaven where nobody spoke and everyone danced, and a holiday was always just about to arrive."

And so I dance.

“After a brief conversation, we parted ways. But I had a feeling about her. About us.”

15

Diamonds Are Forever

For a while I had been watching for her, as she seemed to be at every large party I attended. Always casually chatting with the crowd, hair perfectly coiffed, head tossed back in a gale of laughter. The light seemed to follow her about. She was like diamonds in the sunlight, the center of attention no matter where she moved. Engaging, enchanting, easygoing. She was the antithesis of me.

I wanted to be her friend.

Having been transferred to a giant, glitzy city, I found that making friends outside of our ten-hour days at the office wasn't easy. My very best friend lived five hundred miles away. We had been inseparable for years and continued to visit and work together every chance we got. We were a party of two and had many adventures with our divorces, dating, and daily lives.

I spent every holiday with her large and gracious family, and together we had traveled all over the globe, both strong and independent. Our adventures are book-worthy, and many will provide the best of stories. Someone once wrote, "A good friend knows all your best stories, but a best friend has lived them with you." That was us. We've stayed close to this day. I know she would do anything in the world for me, and I for her.

But I needed a friend in the city where I lived. Of course, I had friends I adored at work, but not the soul-baring, sofa-sleeping, whacked out-weeping kind that could talk me off the ledge over some beguiling, beyond-reach bad boy. I missed that. And anyway, I had a feeling about that amazing, aura-encased girl across the room, the one who sparkled like diamonds.

And I was right.

Months went by before we were introduced. She amazingly approached me one night as I was walking back to my table, dressed in a black, backless cocktail dress. "What on earth have you been doing?" she asked. "Your back looks fabulous." I had no idea my single-girl, time-absorbing weight training actually was even visible. After a brief conversation, we parted ways. But I had a feeling about her. About us.

And I was right.

Months later, as I wandered through another black-tie bash with the same elusive escort, she again appeared, only this time she began a comical conversation with my gentleman friend. And we were finally introduced. Discovering we were both in the advertising/design business, we briefly chatted and then went our separate ways. But then the next week she called me for lunch. And we've been joined at the hip ever since.

It's funny how I always know who I am going to befriend way in advance. It has happened many times in my life, maybe because I am such a people watcher. I sit back and watch, and when I'm sure of my instincts, I do whatever I can to meet that person. That's the way it happened here, although she was the one who valiantly took the lead.

And I was right.

Our lunch went as if we had known each other for years. We were both graphic designers, loved designer clothes, and hated to work out. And as fate would have it, we were even sorority sisters, although we'd gone to school thousands of miles apart. C. S. Lewis wrote," Friendship is born at the moment one person says to another, "What, you too? I thought I was the only one!" That was us. We were going to be friends.

After our meal, and because of my definitely developed and defined back muscles, she decided to join me at the personal training studio for my thrice weekly bloodletting. It was the beginning of our friendship, and after an hour and a half of lunges, weights, and crunches, off we'd go to a calorie-laden home cooking restaurant for dinner. Despite our sinful suppers, we both became firm and fine … something neither of us had been since our twenties. One such evening, as I was ranting about my self-adoring suitor, tears came to her beautiful, blue eyes. We traded secrets and stories, our first really intimate conversation, and left the restaurant solid and secure as sisters, heading home.

We discovered we lived right around the corner from each other.

It was an omen. We were sure. We worked together, we played together, we shared our hopes and dreams together. And we laughed. Oh, how we laughed. And on Sunday evenings, because she was not much of a cook, her hunk of a husband and she would walk over for dinner, where I would proudly serve them my single-girl specialty, a recipe named Chicken Roger. We traveled around the corner and around the world together, and I learned to love her husband as much as I do her.

And then I married.

It couldn't be any other way. Not with them. They accepted and loved my husband as well. No pretense, no boundaries. And that's not easy. How many couples do you find where both partners really like and respect each other? Picking a husband is a dangerous decision when you have a close circle of friends. It changes the dynamic and has frozen many a female friendship. It takes a true friendship, built on trust, patience, and tolerance, to accept someone new into the fold.

That reminds me too of my new husband's introduction to my then boss. He and his partner were like brothers to me, we spent so much time together at work and after. Not knowing my darling's comfort level with my generous and delightfully gay guy friends, I was a bit apprehensive of the evening. After drinks and canapés, we climbed into the back seat of our host's car and proceeded to the restaurant. As we neared the corner, his partner turned toward us, slapped my handsome hubby on the knee and said, "Welcome to the family, precious." We all howled with laughter and formed a foursome that's lasted a lifetime.

Thirty-five years later, across decades, distance, and dramas, my shining sister of sunlight continues to be the one I turn to when I need encouragement, enlightenment, or empathy. She has never wavered; she is always there. We have celebrated victories and weathered repeated losses of parents and jobs and other friends. We have helped glue back together broken hearts as our pets crossed the Rainbow Bridge. And we are each other's protective pillar as we watch our closest colleagues combat cancer and other devastating diseases. We have learned that to lean is to love.

We know someday it will be us.

Now that we've settled halfway across the country from each other, we see one another only once or twice a year. Our memories of events and experiences are some of the best of my life. We've been good together, and we've been bad together. But as with all true friendships, time and distance are no longer factors. And for someone who is sparkling sunlight in a storm, she is easy to spot. And she in turn sees me—the real me. She knows how I've cried over lost loves, and how I laugh when I get nervous. She knows I love English muffins for breakfast, pop culture and fashion, anything that sparkles, and preppie men in Oxford shirts and rep ties. She knows I love to help decorate their Christmas tree and cook for them when I'm in town. She knows I'm always up for mischief and down for a good party where I can dance like it's 1968. She knows too that I love her.

Gina Barreca wrote, "It's not that diamonds are a girl's best friend, but it's your best friends who are your diamonds."

She was right.

"I wanted to see the Haight and the hippies and climb to the top of the seven hills. But more than anything, I wanted to touch the sky."

16

Flowers in My Hair

Linda Ronstadt lived around the corner.

Not that she was my BFF, of course, but her lavender "painted lady" Victorian cloaked in pale pink roses was one of the many, marvelous memories I have of my life in San Francisco. It was a place where I felt most like me.

Our house was a gray Edwardian in Pacific Heights, just at the crest of the hill. "A great space," said our Realtor. And that it was. You could see the glorious Golden Gate Bridge and that breathtaking bay from the deck and flower filled trees from the rest. It is my favorite of all the places in which I have lived.

You see, San Francisco was an absolute assault on my senses.

I never knew a city could smell like flowers. It was intoxicating, invigorating, incredible. And that meant that our home smelled like fragrant, fresh flowers literally all the time. Because the City by the Bay was free of bugs, our super-sized, screen-free, gleaming glass windows were open to the beautiful, brilliant blue sky all day and nearly all nights.

My days began with a walk to the corner to catch the bus to Union Square where I worked. The corner provided an astonishing view of the palatial Palace of Fine Arts, the glorious Golden Gate Bridge, and the bay. It was like looking at a postcard every morning, stamped and delivered to me, come rain or come shine. As the electric bus sauntered soundlessly through the sleeping streets, we passed Alta Plaza, the neighborhood park, where dozens of elegant Asians moved in tandem, like weightless waves, as they delicately danced their daily tai chi.

As we wandered toward the city's center, we passed the dazzling dragons that guard the gleaming geranium gates to Chinatown. Hidden on the next street was the Oriental Pearl, where we spent lazy, rainy Sunday afternoons drinking jasmine tea and eating exotic entrées. The streets were narrow and smelled sweetly of incense. They were illuminated with colorful paper lanterns that danced above our heads like fireworks on the Fourth. There were vivid vegetables, fresh fruit, and silly souvenirs for sale everywhere, and our ears were challenged with chopped Chinese conversations coming from a world so very far away.

It was all so fabulously foreign.

The bus bounded down the steep streets and stopped at Union Square. This was my weekday, workday stop. It was filled with people rushing to their offices. But on the weekends, it was filled with mellow musicians and artists that offered easy conversation and camaraderie. The air smelled of freshly brewed coffee beans and vanilla candles. It was here that I loved to linger and absorb the colors and chords that consumed me. I was filled with a staggering sense of gratitude.

And then there is the bay.

The choppy waters are the glorious gateway to sunny Saturdays in Sausalito. Gazing through galleries, feasting on freshly caught crab salads and smooth Sancerre. Watching the sun set over the city's skyline, as the whitewashed hills, slowly turning gray, prepare for slumber as the fog covers them for the night. As the ferry pulls up to the dock, and we head toward home, a large, luminous moon lights our way.

I will never forget my first time in San Francisco. It was 1970, and I had dreamed of it since college. I wanted to see it. I wanted to go to the Fillmore and hear Jimi, Jackson, and Janis sing my favorite songs. I wanted to see the Haight and the hippies and climb to the top of the seven hills. But more than anything, I wanted to touch the sky.

And I did.

I realized years later that I saw the sights, but I didn't see the city. I didn't walk down the old moneyed, mansion-lined streets, I didn't wade in the waves at Baker Beach or climb the Baker Steps, I didn't dine in the unsigned restaurants packed with locals and hidden in alleyways. I didn't discover beauty in the Presidio's tended trails or the ugly side of life in the Tenderloin. I didn't hear Dylan's lilting lyrics waft through open windows or the crystal clear carillon bells in Union Square play "San Francisco (Be Sure to Wear Flowers in Your Hair)" every evening at six.

Until I did.

I have lived north, south, east, and west and points in between and fallen for almost all of them. But I was a child of the sixties, so San Francisco became an inspiration and major influence on my life. And much like this seven-by-seven spectacular square miles of a city, I am strong and resilient, and gentle and generous. A steel magnolia with flowers in my hair. And while I lost my heart to San Francisco, …

I also found myself.

Now I live in the South, and again I am happy and carelessly content. I eat grits and fried green tomatoes. I belong to a tribe of accomplished and wildly amusing women with whom I share the future. But as I drive around town listening to Sirius soft sixties, I am transported back in time.

And whenever Linda Ronstadt begins to sing, I swear I can smell the roses.

“We traveled on location shoots all over the country together, along with models, photographers, and crews with whom we also formed friendships for life.”

17

Working It Out

I had a stellar career.

I had known at nine exactly what I wanted to do, after seeing the movie *Funny Face*. The beauty of the clothes, the models, the artistic and creative crew—I loved it all.

And so I entered college in the mid-sixties and became the only fashion student in the entire school. That worked to my advantage, as I had no real classes as such, just projects to complete from the head of the department. My senior project included designing a dress, making the pattern, designing and silk-screening the fabric, making the dress, being photographed in the dress, and designing, writing, and then producing the ad.

I loved it and made an A.

I had worked selling clothes and wrapping gifts only in my daddy's store, so I was hesitant to apply for a position at one of the large downtown department stores. As I rode the bus back then, one day it stopped in front of one of the city's finest. In I went with my portfolio of fashion sketches, in a new lavender linen dress. I met with the art director, a lovely and talented man, who hired me that day, mainly because he said I had the most beautiful hair. My position was production artist, something I knew nothing about, yet he promised I would pick it up easily.

I was terrified.

After being trained by the woman who had resigned, I became part of a curious cadre of creatives … artists, writers and designers, with whom I learned so much about the ad business besides enjoying countless evenings of food and fun. We had a great time and literally laughed all day. I couldn't believe I was being paid to work there. I also learned that I was partial to the department jokes and mischief. Being the last to touch any photo or art that went to the engraver for the newspaper ads, I found that I was able to finally wreak revenge on a college colleague who was incredibly mean.

She became head of the store's college fashion board and was featured in a full-page ad, advertising the board's fall fashion show. Needless to say, this was a big deal in college. Everyone was envious. As the photographs were packaged for the engraver, I simply blacked out her two front teeth. When the photo came back in, I quickly wiped off the markings and filed it away. Nobody could figure out what on earth happened, except the few of us who were in hysterics the entire day.

I was full of ideas and was promoted quickly.

Three years later, I was the art director and supervised all the artists and designers. I had a wonderful rapport with my boss and her boss, the vice president of sales promotion. They were in the process of planning the big fall fashion show and wanted me to model the wedding dress, which was always the last glamorous garment on the runway. With that honor, my then-boyfriend and I were to marry onstage, and be treated to an all-expenses-paid Hawaiian honeymoon. My mother was horrified. We thought it was swell. Unfortunately, yet fortunately, I was recruited by another store weeks before the show, and they retracted the offer. Unfazed by this, my tears at leaving were only for the wonderful people I left behind and my bosses who had trained and nurtured me.

I couldn't believe my next set of bosses were even greater. I was lucky to land in a place where I was inspired creatively and trained so well. I began traveling to New York for meetings, learned how to art-direct fashion photography, and honed my design skills. I was quickly promoted again, and eventually became Associate Creative Director to a wonderful man and lifelong friend—and a serious partner in crime. We were always up to mischief in the office, playing jokes and laughing until we couldn't catch our breath. We put Valium in the coffeepot when our boss was driving us nuts, taped anchovies under desks, and removed speakers from telephones. We traveled on location shoots all over the country together, along with models, photographers, and crews with whom we also formed friendships for life. When we shot on location, we were all together for weeks on end. We spent days together working out of a big RV, having catered meals and snacks, and laughing ourselves silly.

Of course, there was lots of work to be done. So when a rain cloud came into view, or a late dress sample didn't arrive by Fed Ex, or someone was having a meltdown, it got really tense. You had to think on your feet. Once, as the sun was going down, I had to talk some young mother in Central Park into letting me dress her little toddler boy up like a girl and take his picture for our catalog. Another time, during shooting out in the desert, a model was bitten on the chest by the horse she was posing with. The male model working with her said, "I'm a doctor; let me see." The photographer asked what kind of a doctor he was, and he snapped, "A veterinarian." We howled.

I couldn't have been more delighted for the opportunity to engage with such a collection of creatives. And despite the drama in the office, and there was a lot of drama, power plays, and politics, we felt fortunate that we were doing what we loved. As the retail environment changed and marketing strategies evolved, bosses were replaced, and budgets tightened, we began to deal with mergers and layoffs and big, big changes. Self-promotion replaced teamwork; money and prestige displaced creative excellence. The business became a bean counter's paradise, and success was measured by sales. Period.

It is obvious that the person above is my all-time favorite advertising boss. He taught me a great deal and even inspired me to write. He was supportive and kind, besides being a bucket of fun. But I have also adored several other bosses, most of all a wonderful woman at Saks, Inc., whom I hold in the utmost respect—brilliant, intuitive, and generous. And the woman who hired me at the Bombay Company. What vision, creativity, and style! And I cannot leave out the CEO of Macy's, an uber-intelligent, inventive, and imaginative man and passionate merchant who astounded me with his wisdom.

Several I would like to string up.

Not for how they treated me, but for all the young artists they influenced along the way. The younger people didn't have the opportunities we had back in the golden days of retail. They didn't realize how creative and innovative retail advertising could be. How you were nurtured and supported and inspired. These bad bosses were culturally different and diverse, yet they had several traits in common, topped by terrible management skills and a totally inflated sense of self. They were relentlessly political. And of course, they thought everyone adored and admired them.

As if.

As my last retail gig blew up in another corporate takeover, I changed careers and became director of communications for a state arts school. I was making less than half my usual salary but enjoying life twice as much. It was stress free, full of vacation time, and a relaxed and creative environment. I was there ten years before I retired and was grateful for the experience.

And best of all, I adored my boss.

"Everyone you touch has a role in your story, and if you let them, they will enrich your life by elevating and enhancing your experiences and opportunities."

18

Unlikely Connections

No one is put in your path by accident.

I am fascinated by human connection, what draws people together, especially unlikely connections. I have made lifelong friendships when delayed in an airport, at work, and at bodacious black-tie disease balls.

It is so interesting that things we have in common—be it our career choice, a past love, or a totally inappropriate and irreverent sense of humor—can bind us to a stranger for decades. I have one friend who amazingly participated in a totally inappropriate yet hilarious string of texts that left us both in cray-cray hysterics for weeks before we actually got together. Our husbands were ready to reserve a room for us at the local psych hospital before we regained our composure and acted somewhat like adults.

We still have our moments.

Unlikely connections are based on random circumstances that, in all fairness, are unusual in today's world. It's like those animal books with stories of a tiger befriending a monkey, or a caring canine raising a squirrel. What draws them together? What quirk of nature makes a bond possible? I, for one, have never wanted to have children. Don't ask me why because I don't even remember making that decision. It always was. And today, most of my close friends, with a very few exceptions, have never wanted or had children either. A physician friend explained it as having extremely low amounts of the hormone oxytocin in our systems. However, most of us have inherited children through our second husbands, which is an interesting twist of fate. These circumstances have produced some horrific and some happy situations.

Of course, when first married, most second brides were ignored at best. Some remain that way today. I am lucky in that I inherited an amazing, adorable, and accomplished stepdaughter with two lady-killer sons, all of whom I love and enjoy being around. For me, they were the icing on the cake. My friends, with one Hallmark Channel movie–worthy exception, have had truly psycho spawns in their homes, with disastrous results. The drama was never-ending. And now that we're older, some spouses are passing away, and there is the inheritance to fight over. What was previously awkward has now become angry.

It ain't no *Father Knows Best*.

Years ago, after countless tales of being excluded and evaded, I formed the Wicked Stepmother's Club. Of course, none of us were really wicked; we were all sociable, smart, savvy women who by circumstance had part-time children become part of our lives. Interestingly, their mothers' biggest fear initially was that we would want to win them over, become another "Mom."

Nothing could be farther from the truth.

Every Christmas, six Wicked Stepmothers and their husbands would come to a formal dinner at our home. We ate, drank, and told stories of Xanax-worthy, frightful family gatherings—the kind where you were the only one without a gift to open. It became funny actually, who would win the Holiday Horror Story of the evening. This party was one of the highlights of the Christmas season for all of us. And through the years, the parent-child relationships have evolved. Some for better, some for worse. But the good news now is that those former teenagers and tykes are now adults and responsible for their decisions and actions. This makes it much easier on us. There is no guilt for what isn't.

And gratitude for what is.

All of the Wicked Stepmothers are confident and self-sufficient, regardless of their new husbands. All of them, when faced with the "fight or flight" scenario with their previous husbands, chose the latter. I like them because they're feisty, a take-no-prisoners group of gals. They're the ones who years ago were tersely told, "You'll never find anyone like me again."

"That's the idea," they all replied.

These ladies have moved on. But where they landed gifted them with new family dynamics, and each was automatically pitted against the First Wife, usually described as a cold, ruthless woman with a dour sense of humor who spent all her time shopping. It almost comes as a prerequisite that the New Wife not like the First Wife, and vice versa. She hears stories of alimony, child support, and all the "never enough" financial complaints coming his way. The Ex-Wife hears stories about the New Wife from the kids. It's betrayal for them to accept the poor woman, much less like her. It's all so complicated.

Until it isn't.

Until the day everyone puts their hurt feelings and anger aside, they can't realize that we are all just trying to be happy. We are all in this together. We share a history, albeit fractured, but at some point in our lives we all cared for each other.

It took my husband's sweet father dying to throw me in with his ex. I flew from New York, where I was working at the time, to his funeral in Louisiana. The very last to arrive, I just knew everyone was waiting for the fireworks. There were whispers of "When's Peggi coming?" throughout the day. We all stayed at the same hotel and finally ended up in the bar one evening, talking and telling stories until midnight.

And I learned she was lovely.

My sister and I are friendly with our exes from Texas, too. When I returned to Dallas for a high school reunion, we all had dinner together, new wives and all. We laughed ourselves silly at stories from when we all shared an apartment in the 1970s. We were fresh from college and starting our careers and learning to cook and be responsible, all at the same time. There are memories that made us laugh until tears ran down our now wrinkled faces, even the new wives, who have obviously heard them before. And there was the awkward family photo of my father smiling into the camera one Thanksgiving dinner, with my ex-brother-in-law lurking in the background in a gorilla mask. My Wasband tells me he wants me to meet his daughter. "She reminds me of you," he says, "with a thousand pair of shoes." And his new wife thanks me for all I have given her, especially the grandfather clock and her hubby. We laugh. I tell her she is perfect for him—much more his type. She loves the outdoors, the beach, and fishing, and all his passions. When we talk of the great outdoors, she thinks adventure. I think *Deliverance*.

We are so different in some ways and so alike in others.

We have become Facebook friends and are there to support each other as we learn to grow old. We have an understanding of each other through our shared history. It is an unlikely connection, but one I enjoy.

We are Sister Wives.

In this dangerously digital world of hashtags, influencers, and followers, we must acknowledge the importance of human connection. Being a Boomer, I am glad I didn't grow up glued to my iPhone. We had to talk to people, and we learned how to connect in a meaningful way. Superficial connectedness appears to be the preference of millennials, as technology threatens to replace face-to-face intimacy. With devices in hand, we can totally avoid human exchange, and its potential awkwardness. It makes me wonder if they will all be living in isolation when they grow old.

What a terrible thought.

I don't know what I'd do without my friends. I am so fortunate to have a bunch, and the collective group is very diverse. Some are crazy artists, some physicians, some pedagogues, some straight, some gay, some young enough to be my children. It's an unconventional mix, much like a great pot of gumbo. The result is quite extraordinary. But the thing they have in common is that there is a history with each of them, whether a time, trouble, or triumph. And my unlikely friends share a piece of history too. Some random event at some point in time, knowledge of people I once loved, places where I once lived or worked.

They make the mix so much better.

So whether they're Sister Wives, Stepmothers, or Besties, I consider connecting with others one of the greatest joys in life. It makes you part of something much bigger than yourself, a collective consciousness of conversations, challenges, and cherished memories that create our own history. Everyone you touch has a role in your story, and if you let them, they will enrich your life by elevating and enhancing your experiences and opportunities. The magic comes from our similarities and differences with unique people who make an indelible impression on us. Or they offer us the opportunity to know ourselves better. It's a win-win. All our connections define who we are.

So don't be judgmental.

No one is perfect. We are all pieces in a great universal picture puzzle, each of us unique. When we find our place, where we are supposed to be, we become connected to something bigger than ourselves. And that vast visual is made up of random, irregular, misshapen parts that alone are perfectly imperfect.

In some way, every one of us is messed up. Everyone has issues, some more than others. Some wear them on their sleeve, some bury them under layer upon layer of airtight armor. They are waiting for you to discover them, to reveal them, to revel in them. It's what makes this journey called life more interesting. So pick your favorite train wreck.

And roll with it.

"Every time I hear the Kinks, the Byrds, the Beatles—oh, could I go on—I am back at those parties doing the boogaloo, the push, and the jerk or leading line dances with absolute abandon."

19

Personal Playlists

Behind every favorite song is a story.

I am almost embarrassed to mention that whenever I hear the Rolling Stones' "Satisfaction," I am immediately transported back to 1964 and Dallas's Memorial Auditorium on New Year's Eve, dancing the dirty dog with my first boyfriend. I have on a burgundy and white tweed sleeveless wool minidress with a low-slung burgundy leather belt, white pantyhose, and my collegiately cool Weejuns. We are drinking Scotch and dancing to the Hot Nuts. Over my left breast, barely visible I might add, is my sorority Ideal Pledge pin, something I wear with pride as being voted the favorite pledge among my pledge class. Seven months prior I had graduated as a totally invisible and inconspicuous individual in a high school class of almost a thousand seniors.

You've come a long way, baby.

I honestly don't know exactly what snapped when my sister and I entered college. Maybe our home was more oppressive than we realized. Or maybe the fact that everyone entering college was new leveled the playing field from being the new girls in high school. Whatever it was, we ran with it. As we dated for literally the first time in our lives, the constant fraternity parties with live dance bands became the center of our world. We both loved to dance and were good dancers. And of course, the music scene exploded in the mid-sixties.

Every time I hear the Kinks, the Byrds, the Beatles—oh, could I go on—I am back at those parties doing the boogaloo, the push, and the jerk or leading line dances with absolute abandon. Whenever "Brown-Eyed Girl" comes on the radio, I think of my college roommate; when Cream sings "Sunshine of Your Love," I remember my cute college boyfriend and his Sigma Chi pin I wistfully wore on my chest.

What is it about music?

Fast forward to the seventies when I fell in love to Dylan's "Lay, Lady, Lay," and later settled into our first home to Crosby, Stills, Nash & Young's "Our House." We purchased that adorable Tudor at just the right time in just the right place. Its stained-glass windows and hardwood floors were secondary to its location, called the "M Streets" in Dallas. It was the beginning of my love of remodeling old homes but unfortunately the ending of my marriage. I divorced my then-husband years later to Chicago's "If You Leave Me Now." Which I did.

Each memory has a soundtrack of its own.

The day my mother passed away, a complete and total surprise, my Wasband picked me up at the office and drove me home. I don't remember much about that day except that during the drive, I was haunted all the way home by Led Zeppelin's song "Stairway to Heaven." It was sad and haunting, much like a funeral dirge. To this day it makes my stomach clench.

Fortunately, when I think of my mom, I mostly remember those tender tunes "Moon River" and "True Love," which she played incessantly on the trendy console hi-fi in our living room. It's no wonder that *Breakfast at Tiffany's* and *High Society* are my favorite old movies. When I think of my dad, I hear Noel Coward's "Room with a View" playing in my head. I heard his record albums throughout my youth, and I still remember the words to all of his songs.

After being granted a divorce, and with fire in my belly, I sped seductively around Dallas in my Fiat Spider convertible playing the soundtrack to *American Gigolo*, with "Call Me" loudly blaring in my tape deck. I can conjure up a picture of myself wearing my white Ralph Lauren linen dress with a navy grosgrain ribbon belt, the same color as my car, speeding down Central Expressway to meet a boyfriend for lunch. It was a moment of complete and utter freedom. Exhilaration at its best.

And Blondie provided the soundtrack.

Memorable lovers, with automatically assigned songs, filled the next fifteen years. I danced with strangers at various North Dallas mixers, always to Foreigner's "I've Been Waiting for a Girl like You," which seemed to be the cattle call for the curious. I went weekly with my girlfriends just to prove to myself that I was making an effort to meet people instead of curling up at home with my books. I was terrible at the whole singles scene, and to this day, that track sends shivers down my spine.

Singers and songwriters were as varied as my faceless dates, but hearing just a few notes of some familiar score conjures vivid visions of each one. From the soulful Spinners, to the earth-shattering Eagles, songs and lyrics marked the days and lays of my life. I'm afraid my brain is 85 percent song lyrics. To this day, I astound my husband with the ability to sing every song on the car radio.

What is it about music?

If you ever spent any time in San Francisco, you would automatically think of the beautiful bells playing at dusk in Union Square. Hearing the tune "San Francisco" was a magical and melodic memory as I walked through the square every night from my office to the bus stop that would take me up the hill to Pacific Heights. I knew I was late to the bus stop by the absence of the song. Why is this so clear in my seventy-three-year-old mind?

I've done a little snooping.

Dartmouth researchers have learned that the part of the brain that handles information from your ears, holds on to musical memories. The researchers also found that lyrics impact the various brain regions that are called upon when musical memories are recounted. What happens is that a piece of familiar music serves as a soundtrack for a mental movie that starts playing in our heads. You might all of a sudden see that person's face in your mind's eye. Now we can see the amazing association between the music and the memories.

I love that we are full of soundtracks—personal playlists all our own.

If anyone is familiar with English singer/songwriter James Blunt, you'll be familiar with lyrics he wrote to a song that was a profound soundtrack to one of my life's onerous events. I had become obsessed with his second album, *All the Lost Souls*. It would play in my car for weeks on end. One of his ballads, the tender "Carry You Home," was my favorite, although deeply moving and somewhat depressing. At the time, my wonderful, wonky Wheaten Terrier, Ollie, was getting on in years, and I could see that his days were numbered. He was lethargic and looked lost.

My heart was broken.

Toward the end, on the way to work one day, I had carried him to my incredibly kind veterinarian for a bath. As he met us in the waiting area, he took one look at Ollie and paused. Looking straight into my eyes, he whispered, "It's time." We decided I would come back at the end of the day to say goodbye and stay with him while he was put down. I was a mess. As I drove to work, my radio played "Stairway to Heaven."

My stomach clenched. My day was a million hours long. And then it was time.

Ollie's tail wagged as I entered the room. I remember the *thump-thump-thump* it made. My vet and I sat with him on the floor. I pulled him into my lap and told him I loved him. After the peaceful procedure was over, I left Ollie to be cremated and began the trip home. I was in such shock I couldn't begin to cry. It's that feeling that if you start, you may never recover. So off I went heading toward home. About halfway there, James Blunt came on the radio. It happened to be the tearful track "Carry You Home." It totally broke me as I listened to the lilting lyrics.

That was 2009. And I haven't listened to it since.

"I hope, however, they aren't able to look into my past and see the pots of delicious dove gumbo I cooked as a young housewife."

The Visitors

I've never really liked birds.

Lately, I have been wondering why these two tiny mourning doves keep coming back, year after year, to our balcony. Last night, they sat and stared at me for over an hour. It is starting to give me the creeps.

I may be the preteen product of Hitchcock's harrowing tale starring Tippi Hedren. His movie *The Birds* was more than frightening and sparked a cult following that included my sister. One Halloween, she purchased and wore a Tippi costume complete with six stuffed blackbirds sewn to it—and another sewn onto the jaunty little hat. It was the best.

I have never owned a bird.

My grandfather had a pampered, pale blue pet parakeet named Budgey, who frighteningly flew out his Manhattan apartment window once during a family visit. We were all horrified. He was heartbroken. I knew then you just can't trust them. And then there's all the superstition about birds. That they come when someone is about to die. Or that cardinals are visiting dead spirits. Jeez.

But then I do have a good bird story.

My mother had just died, and I was lying on the couch of my first big-girl apartment. I was incredibly sad, shocked, and soulfully singed to my core. I kept talking to my mom in my muddled, mourning mind. "Give me a sign, please; just give me a sign that you are all right." Eventually I fell asleep from exhaustion. Suddenly, I heard a persistent pecking at my patio door. Lo and behold, a waxen white dove was staring at me through the glistening glass door. *Peck, peck, peck.* Pecking and staring straight into my eyes. *Peck, peck, peck.*

I knew that was my sign.

Which brings me back to these little brown doves. I look for them now daily. Sometimes they come in a pair, sometimes alone. But they always come, year after year, and I wonder why. Their call is a distinctive *wooo-oo-oo-oo*, which sounds very sad and evokes a feeling of grief and loneliness. But beyond their sorrowful song, per the internet, their message is a message of life, hope, renewal, peace, and safety. A fitting message for these weird and wacky times.

So now I am wondering what to feed them.

I hope, however, they aren't able to look into my past and see the pots of delicious dove gumbo I cooked as a young housewife. My Wasband was outrageously outdoorsy, something my friends now would never believe, and he would return home with bags upon bags bursting with little dove breasts begging to be braised. I never really fancied the dish, but in my youthful exuberance at entertaining, I smiled and scooped out bountiful bowls to all our many friends. They were joyful. I have also come home to a bathtub filled with piles of pale, panting fish, woefully waiting to be filleted. That made my friends even happier.

But that's another story.

One of my favorite music icons, Stevie Nicks, was inspired by doves when she wrote her hit "Edge of Seventeen." She was flying home from Phoenix, Arizona, in the early eighties and was handed a menu that said, "The white wing dove sings a song that sounds like she's singing ooh, ooh, ooh." Seems the doves made their home in the surrounding hills. Nicks had never actually heard a dove's song until she recently heard the sound of a bird singing the same thing repeatedly. One little "ahhh," and then three "whos" over and over again. She thought it was an owl, but a friend told her it was a dove, bringing her to tears. She thought the dove had come to watch over her.

I am totally in sync with Stevie.

So that's what I have come to believe. That darling, delicate, dove duo are here to wordlessly, wondrously watch over me. Year after year, they return to my little balcony overlooking the gorgeously green park across the road. They spend their spring and summer nesting and making babies and watching me day after day. And now I watch for them.

I've begun to ponder their pattern.

Their comings and goings are like clockwork. They keep their appointments and are rarely late. Clearly, they don't just wing it. They have a relentless routine and a piercing perseverance.

They are determined and diligent. And when they are sure that all's right with my world, their time with us is done. Then the clock strikes twelve, they fly elsewhere, to another world where they are needed, and their aquiline attention graces another life.

Where do they go? I have no idea. Why do they come? I have no idea. Are they mystical messengers from another world? I have no idea.

Who, who, who.

"She was the epitome of the daughter I never had, but would select if asked."

Hello, I'm Katie

She said her name was Katie.

The earnest young lady sitting across from my desk was strategically styled for her interview. White severely starched shirt, pleated plaid skirt, big "I mean business" black glasses perched on her perfectly powdered nose. Her skin was like porcelain, her hair long, straight, and blond since birth. Willowy and weightless, she was adorable, and could have just wandered out of a J.Crew catalog. She was the epitome of the daughter I never had, but would select if asked.

Ambitious and wise beyond her years, Katie had cold-called and asked if I ever hired interns. I hadn't but realized I certainly could and invited her in for a chat. A marketing major at UAB, she needed real world experience for her senior project. As our interview ended and we were saying our goodbyes, she leaned across the desk and touched my hand in gratitude.

Totally smitten, I hired her on the spot.

She was a strong writer, an independent thinker, and easily earned her place among the office staff. Composed, introspective and inquisitive, Katie was amazingly astute at seeking out the best in people and telling their stories in a genuine, graceful way. Katie was a people person and loved stories.

Katie loved my stories. And I loved hers.

Born to a faith-based family that was light-years away from mine, Katie traveled the world like global warming. Her mom was a flight attendant, and as soon as Katie and I became frequent Facebook friends, I was awed by the photos of her riding horses on the Argentinian beaches, bundled in blankets in Antarctica, and daringly diving off the cliffs of County Clare.

She has been to almost all places overseas we've heard of and most of the places we haven't. I couldn't imagine such a fearless and undaunted soul writing press releases and magazine articles all day in an office.

She came to her senses having her morning coffee at Lucy's.

Her early morning routine included eavesdropping on her colleagues' conversations at her favorite coffee shop. One day she tiptoed into my office, sat down, and softly said, "I think I'm going to go to medical school and become a doctor."

"You'll be a great one," I replied. With that she gently touched my hand, smiled, and went on about her day.

It seems that for weeks her morning regimen had awakened her to the fact that medicine was much more interesting than communications. So soon after graduation, and the end of her internship, Katie applied to med school and then shortly left for a summer job at a youth hostel in Amsterdam. Her duties included running the front desk and riding her bike to the local market, where she purchased and then prepared breakfast for the residents.

She had never cooked in her life.

Of course this didn't stop her. After a few mornings of mysterious menus, Katie developed a series of meals that required little cooking. When her tenure came to a close, and she hadn't heard if she was admitted to med school yet, Katie decided to become a flight attendant.

Actually, the good news arrived the same day she left for Delta flight training. Delaying her education for a year, she earned her wings and immediately relocated to New York. She loved flying. She met interesting people. She made lifelong friends. Weekends were spent as a standby passenger to points unknown, even if it meant having dinner in Dubai but skipping dessert to catch her free flight back to the States. And all this time, she wrote me letters: letters from London, letters from Marrakesh, letters that stamped her fingerprint on my heart. She returned home and started studying medicine.

Katie is now in her last year at UAB and excelling. As she describes her daily experiences, I am amazed at the empathy she exhibits and the lessons learned about the frailty of life. She again touched my hand across the dinner table and tenderly told me that she cries every day. She can't imagine ever stopping.

I told Katie recently that I hope her path is primary care so she could take care of me when my days on this earth are ending.

Pausing, she looked me in the eye and wrinkled her faintly freckled nose. Then once again she reached across the table and thoughtfully touching my blueberry stained, heavily veined hand and said that she'd most likely choose the ER.

But she promised she would be there and hold my hand.

“You need to marry this girl. She has a great sense of humor.”

22

A Love Story

I am hopelessly in love.

I'm in love with my life, my dashing and darling husband, my ridiculously adorable rescue dog. I am surrounded by amazing art, best-selling books, a gentrified and gloriously green-hilled city, a cadre of accomplished and accepting friends and a sensational sister who gets me since we've been joined at the hip since birth. And despite a wonky childhood and a few challenges along the way, sometimes I want to pinch myself for being where I am at this very moment. To say I'm grateful is an understatement.

Oh yes, I have regrets. A failed first marriage with someone I don't even recognize today. Who was that underweight, overwhelmed girl child? A cracked cartoon statue destined to disintegrate at any moment. I was shattered by loss … loss of my mother, my father and my incredible innocence. I was disillusioned and walking a tight wire. And no one knew.

Just me.

Fast-forward to years of post-divorce dating. Oh my God, those men. Now granted, I had a really great time. I dated some fantastic guys, some not so much, as I had a corner on those emotionally unavailable types. Yes, I know, leftovers from my distant daddy issues. But it wasn't until a Friday night blind date in Dallas that my world changed overnight. I never knew that love at first sight really existed or even what fated, full-throttle love felt like. It was undoubtedly the best night of my life.

He was gorgeous in his tux, with a movie star mug to boot. Charming, captivating, a perfect gentleman. We dined, we danced. Oh, could he dance. We talked and giggled and stayed out until three a.m. I couldn't believe a date, much less a blind date, could be so incredibly perfect. My bestie discovered him and set us up, so the cards were somewhat stacked. She knew me better than anyone and was totally fixated on my best interests. He was totally fixated on me.

Just me.

I went back to work that next Monday and told my close colleague and confidant that I was going to marry him. I just knew it. Later that day, a dozen "you impressed me" yellow roses showed up, bright as the Southern sun. I tore open the enclosed note peeking from between the long, stiff stems. The message gushed. He had a great time "on Saturday night," he said. He wanted to see me again very soon. Unfortunately, I had been out with him on Friday night.

So what's a girl to do?

I purposely picked up the phone and ordered a dozen, long stemmed yellow roses to be delivered to his testosterone-infested investment banker's office with a well-penned note. Now I might add here that he was the single-guy seduction story of the office. Girls calling him all the time, and dropping in to say "Hi" and hoping for another dinner date. HIs sexy secretary, a former Dallas Cowboys cheerleader, was well versed on how to field the friendly female calls and hide him away in the office when necessary. The whole place knew about this blind date, noteworthy news during the constant coffee chatter and after-work drinks dialogue.

They knew he had sent the roses. They were waiting for my call.

They waited and waited. Cocktail conversation consoled him. "The roses were late. She was working outside the office. She wasn't feeling well." Anything to break the stony silence of the office phones. They decided to call it a day and see what tomorrow might bring. A call, for sure.

The morning market was busy, and the office was buzzing. Suddenly, a courier came through the gleaming glass doors with a delightful delivery of a dozen long-stemmed yellow roses. Everyone assumed they were for one of the female assistants, but as the confusion commenced, they made their way back to the mahogany masked offices with the Persian rugs and city views. The cheer captain saw them land on her desk, but thinking they looked way too familiar, she ran to see if they had been mistakenly delivered or returned. A hush fell over the office. They were for him, her boss, her totally smitten, single, starry-eyed boss. A curious crowd gathered outside his door, sympathy stamped on their stoic faces. No one spoke.

Just her.

As she politely placed the festive flowers on his desk, he looked up in shock, then confusion. "Open it," she said. With furrowed brow he took the little white card from its envelope. Slowly tearing the crisp, white flap, he paused and took a deep breath. *This is going to be bad*, he thought. Then he extracted the card and began to read the short, typed message.

"I am so glad you had such a great time Saturday night. Unfortunately, I was with you on Friday night. Does Alzheimer's run in your family?"

He howled.

As he gathered himself and read the flirtatious message aloud, everyone died laughing. They were high-five hand slapping and two-hand clapping and passing on the news. All was well in Single World. It became the giggle of the day. His heart remained intact. His boss came by later that afternoon and read my note.

"You need to marry this girl. She has a great sense of humor."

And so he did. Seven months later, after every weekend in an airport so we could see each other, we finally flew to Maui and married at the gloriously grand Hana Ranch. On a misty day, in a loggia overgrown with orchids, by a Tiffany blue pool of water, we were joined together by a Hawaiian minister and a rented witness. We couldn't understand a word he said. It was the perfect wedding for us. And because it was New Year's Eve, there was a colossal celebration that evening, with a seated dinner, dancing, and dialogue only in German because of our ill-fated table assignments. We couldn't understand a word they said either. But it didn't matter, for just like that Friday evening seven months prior, we dined and danced, and we never took our eyes off each other. I knew what he saw, and I knew it was all he wanted.

Just me.

"What is the soup du jour?" I asked.

"Soup of the day," she replied.

23

Soup du Jour

I was recently the recipient of an article from *The New York Times* containing essays of five writers' best meals in memory. It got me to thinking. And I decided it was not always the fabulous food that made a meal memorable for me, but the experience itself. The greatest gastronomical gems were more about who I was with, what happened, or where I happened to be—as in the amazing conversation I had with one waitress. "What is the soup du jour?" I asked. "Soup of the day," she replied. It really happened. It was all we could do not to burst out in laughter. You can't make these things up.

So I've narrowed my rantings down to the three most memorable meals of my lifetime. Not the fanciest, or the most exotic of world locations, or even those with the sexiest suitors of my past. Just those three times I will never forget, which are just as visually and viscerally vivid today as when they happened.

Vivande, San Francisco, California

We had just flown into San Francisco Airport with our close friends; the four of us gloriously glamping at a friend's Pacific

Heights flat close to where we had lived a few years before. Exhausted from our trip, and seriously starving, I might add, we headed down to Fillmore Street to our favorite Italian grocery store–café, Vivande Porta Via. As we entered the small but spectacular space, we were immediately surrounded by the arresting aroma of glorious grilled garlic and fresh, yeasty Italian bread. Grabbing one of the half dozen, white clothed tables, we settled in for what we assumed would be a quick but luscious lunch.

Luscious was right on, but quick, not so much. After a glass of our favorite red wine and that brilliant bread dipped in the most gratifying, garlic–infused olive oil, we ordered our lunch. I had my favorite Insalata Mista and a plus-size plate of Aglio e Olio. I don't remember what everyone else had, as I was so immersed in the authentic ability of owner and chef Carlo Middione, who had opened up this little piece of heaven in the 1980s.

It was, without question, the best meal I have ever had in my life.

Matter of fact, there was no conversation as we all gobbled up our meals of freshly made pasta as if we hadn't eaten in weeks. As the wine flowed and the time passed, we realized we had been there over three hours, trying tidbits of small plates and devilish desserts as they came floating out of the kitchen. We four couldn't have had a more sensational start to our weeklong stay in the City by the Bay. Even now, as we sit and reminisce about our many travels and experiences together over the last three decades, Vivande always comes up. It was a magical memory for us all.

In a terrible twist of fate, as Bob Dylan once wrote, Chef Middione was in a 2009 auto accident which left him without any smell or taste sensation. They held out hope that his senses would return, but to no avail. That eventually forced him to close Vivande in 2015. It was a shock throughout the neighborhood, as food fans were greeted by a teary goodbye letter taped to the once bustling café door as Vivande bade its neighborhood farewell.

Steak and Ale, Dallas, Texas

I know you are wondering why in the world I would choose Steak and Ale as one of the top five memorable meals. For those of you who haven't had the S&A experience, it was a chain restaurant from back in the 1970s that everyone frequented when they were young and hungry for a big ole steak. And along with your gloriously grilled, melt-in-your-mouth meat and bulbous baked potato ("with everything" if you so desired), you were entitled to the all-you-can-eat, cabin cruiser–sized salad bar.

So coming off a long day of photographing Lord knows what, my photographer bestie and I, tired and tuckered to the bone, decided what we needed was a big rare steak and a good night's sleep. Off we went to Steak and Ale, mecca of big bovine bounty. After being seated and ordering a much-needed glass of red wine, we were approached by our waiter, a nervous young man obviously undone by his first night on the job. We recounted our wish for a succulent, seasoned, savory steak, paired with a big, buttery baked potato "with everything." He thanked us and then said the well-rehearsed line, "Help yourself to the salad bar." Neither of us were interested in salad, so we sat patiently waiting for our meal. We ordered a second glass of wine thinking our meal would arrive shortly. The waiter was running about, trying to keep up with his other patrons, but ultimately brought us the wine. We smiled graciously and took the wine. As we finished that second glass of Cabernet, we tried to get his attention. We had been there well over an hour at this point, so we were sure our steaks were sitting somewhere outside the kitchen cold as ice. Finally, he rushed over. We inquired about our steaks. "Oh," he quipped, "I don't put in the order until after you've eaten your salad."

We were speechless.

After telling him we didn't want a salad, the waiter explained the steak order is always turned in with the salad plates, and we needed to eat a salad in order for him to place our order. Now keep in mind we had worked a ten-hour day and were in no mood to argue. We did try but to no avail. Finally I got up, went to the salad bar, put two crisp lettuce leaves on two chilled plates, and returned to our table. If we hadn't been so tired, we would have been hysterical. As the place thinned out, the dinner crowd leaving for parts unknown, our ludicrously left-brained waiter sauntered back to our table. "Finished already?" he asked.

We gave him the stink eye.

Finally, our meal came, delicious as ever, and afterward, satiated and sleepy, we went our separate ways—never to return for the Steak & Ale experience again.

Nuit du Jour, New York, New York

This was an evening of magic. One of those evenings that make you pinch yourself to be sure you aren't dreaming. Again, after working a long, hot, and sweaty day shooting fashion around the fountain in Central Park, our fabulous French photographer invited us to dinner at eight at his favorite bistro in the Village. He knew the owner and was able to secure a large round table in the tiny establishment for the crew, who were deliriously happy about the invitation.

Arriving early, I popped into a small antique store next to the arty, awe inspiring Nuit du Jour. Recently, I had attended a fundraiser at a Houston mega-mansion with my boss and close friend, where we saw poised on a marble mantel a single sensational silver flute. It was so beautifully artful, we were both mesmerized by the simplicity of it all. As I wandered through the decorative antiques, I spotted another sensational silver flute for sale. I quickly grabbed it as a gift for my boss, knowing he would be overwhelmed with surprise and happiness.

It was time for dinner.

At eight o'clock I wandered into the restaurant and met our lovely French photographer and his assistants for dinner. After the traditional two-cheek kiss, I explained why I was carrying a silver flute, and being a friend of my boss, he thought it was "magnifique." Actually, people all over the small restaurant thought so too, including a remarkably pale Andy Warhol who melted into the white table linens to my right. After a beautiful bowl of flavorful French onion soup, then an amazing meal, followed by a dessert of my favorite profiteroles and a great deal of wine, the crowd became louder and looser and began asking about my flute. It was being passed and admired table to table, as people began bidding on my flute. One gentleman offered me ten times what I had paid, but I held on to it. We laughed and laughed at what a hit it was. The evening was one in a million, but I couldn't wait to fly home and present my gift.

I waited for his birthday.

Weeks went by and then the day finally came. He looked at the long, thin box wrapped and tied with a soft satin ribbon and couldn't imagine what was inside. As he unwrapped the intriguing instrument, and looked at me with obvious confusion, I realized my biggest nightmare had come true. He had no idea why I was giving him a flute.

He had totally forgotten about the beautiful flute we had seen at the party and was, shall we say, underwhelmed by it all. Of course he was grateful for the remembrance and was such a close friend that he immediately placed it on his mantel with gratitude. I was equally grateful for the enchanting evening that single silver flute allowed me and the many times this memory of fabulous food, the fondest of friendship, and a single silver flute has made my heart sing.

But there's more.

I have thought of many more evenings that should be on the list. Among them is my surprise fiftieth birthday arranged by my adorable husband at Angeluna in Fort Worth, where my dearest friends from all over the state celebrated half a century of me. Then my sixtieth, hosted by my bestie, where friends from all over the country danced with abandon to my favorite songs. And our evening at our San Fran neighborhood Osteria, where my hubby went into a surreal MS syndrome where he turned to exit and literally spun all over the restaurant like an unhinged top, leaning over tables of stunned patrons, silencing the entire place until he spun on out the revolving door.

That was the last time we went to Osteria.

There have been so many good times, good meals, good memories, many of which began and ended in a restaurant, whether high-end or a down-home. But many happened at the houses of our wonderful friends and in our own home, a testament to people sharing affection by preparing lovely meals, a way of nurturing those we love. I love to cook and entertain, to have people over. To make things pretty and flavorful, to sit with each other across a table and share a meal with family and friends. It makes me grateful for all I have, an abundance we should all pass on to those less fortunate.

César Chávez once said, "If you really want to make a friend, go to someone's house and eat with him–the people who give you their food give you their heart."

So please, come for dinner.

“After a few handfuls of ground lamb and lentils, I caught my sister’s eye. It was that look—that pre-hysteria, ‘I am really trying to control my face’ look. My lips curled, and I was gone.”

Hysteria

I'm sure my mother thought she had spawned Rosemary's baby.

My sister, at about four years of age, had just fallen down the stairs. It sounded like a sack of potatoes, the *thump-thump-thumping*, except for the shrill screams pouring from her tiny rosebud lips. She had on forest green corduroy overalls, a lovely combination with a pale green T-shirt and her ravishing red ringlets. I remember our outfits were always alike but different in color.

And I was laughing hysterically at the whole scene.

Our mother came charging from the kitchen, wooden spoon in hand, to see what on earth was happening. As she saw my sister in a pint-sized puddle at the foot of the stairs, screaming her head off, she quickly swatted me with the spoon and told me to stop it. *Now.*

"Why are you laughing?" she yelled.

Actually, I didn't know. It just came out. And that's my first memory of laughing uncontrollably at inappropriate times, something I do to this day. Of course, I have researched it. I asked my primary care physician, Dr. Google. At first, I mistakenly asked about "hysterical laughing," which netted a response about mental illness and early-onset dementia. That can't be me. So I changed it to "inappropriate laughter" which netted a much more palatable paragraph about an unconscious coping strategy to stress and anxiety. Seems the laughter not only physically relieves the stress but also is a diversion to fear or feeling uncomfortable.

As a preteen, I did it in church. My sister and I and a few friends would attend the service after our Pioneer Sunday school class. We carried school pictures in our wallets back then; little black-and-white head shots that were sincerely signed "Love ya" by the owner. We traded them like baseball cards, always vying for the cheerleaders and beauties so our collection was considered cool, and we could pretend that we were too. Of course, our collection had its share of nonessential classmates so it provided fantastic fodder for fun. We would pass them back and forth and hide them in the hymnals, which upon discovery would send us spiraling into a gale of laughter. One Sunday we were so OOC (out of control) that my mother was utterly horrified, and even more embarrassed, by our bad behavior.

She read us the riot act on the way home.

In college, I would sometimes lose control during our serious sorority meetings which happened once a week. Our end of the hallowed house hallway was notoriously named The In Crowd, an embarrassingly exclusive club within a club. At meetings, when any outsider spoke whom we had deemed stuck-up and decided not to like, we would all break down in silent, shoulder-shaking hysteria until our extravagant eye makeup and fabulous false eyelashes were running down our faces. Serious sorority secrets would literally send us over the edge, and many a time during a solemn ceremony, I would lose it at the sight of some stern-faced sister with a plant wrapped around her head.

And then I supposedly grew up.

Fortunately, my favorite boss was prone to this same affliction. Our particular predispositions, mixed with the super-sized stress we worked under, were the catalyst for many inappropriate incidents. We also shared a rather sick and sardonic sense of humor, which hardly helped matters. One day after having lunch, we decided to wander about a local five-and-dime store before we headed back to the salt mines. Somehow we ended up in the ladies' undergarment aisle, where my boss happened on the biggest brassiere we had ever seen. I mean both our heads wouldn't fill the gigantic double whatever cups. The sight of this set us off. We started laughing and we just couldn't stop. He decided we needed to purchase it since we were working on our fall fashion campaign, headlined Fashion Giants. We were doubled over and keening by this point with tears cascading down our cheeks. And since I was the girl, he decided I had to take it to the catatonic cashier for purchase.

I got in line.

Now by this time I had zero control over the contortions my face was making; it had developed a life of its own. My cheeks were covered in black eyeliner, and my mouth was stretched over my teeth in a glee-filled grimace, much like Mister Ed, the talking horse. I just couldn't stop. Every time I looked at my boss, hysterically crying across the store, I would lose total control. I'm sure the poor cashier thought I was drunk or on the best of drugs. We finally got out of the store and headed back to the office.

But it didn't stop there.

Locked in his office, we were screaming and on the verge of hyperventilating. When we took it out of the bag, it started all over again. Deciding what to do with this matron's monstrosity was our next hilarious hurdle. And that set off a new wave of wailing. Amazingly, we thought the best thing to do was pack it up in an interstore mail envelope and send it to one of the company's vice presidents anonymously under the title Fashion Giants. So off it went to the executive offices where it became one of many mad memories we still share to this day.

One night I treated my hysteria to dinner.

Actually, my sister and I took our father out to dinner at a Moroccan restaurant in Houston. He loved Indian and Mideastern cuisine, having grown up with it in the UK. Always a natty dresser, he showed up in a tweedy wool jacket and his perennial silk foulard ascot. It must have been a hundred degrees.

Now let me preface this, to any of you who don't know me too well. My relationship with my dad was awkward at best. He was more or less a stranger to me, devoid of affection and consequence. My relationship with him was closer than that of my sister, as I was his favorite, being the artistic one. To make things even more difficult, he was hard of hearing, so conversation was arduous and somewhat annoying. He tended to just talk, not understanding what conversation was happening at the time.

As if there was one.

Daddy was short in stature and walked aided by a cane. His eyesight was failing so he also wore eyeglasses. Unfortunately they were similar to those worn by Elton John. He was quite the character.

Being around him was stressful for us, not only because of our strained relationship, but because we had no idea what to talk about. And then when we did, he couldn't hear us. We should have popped a Valium ahead of time.

I had made reservations without checking the place out. That was my big mistake although I will give the place an A+ for authenticity. We were seated at a low round table. Low is the operative word here. Adding to the discomfort were the round leather hassocks on which we sat—or tried to sit. They were rather slippery, and staying put was a good workout for the old core muscles.

The waitstaff brought the appetizers with large goblets of wine. I recognized the hummus and the little kalamata olives, but not much else. So I turned my attention to the wine. After ordering a lamb dish I have never heard of, we settled in for our stressful supper. We kept drinking as one does when uncomfortable and not in conversation. Finally, the entrée was served. Actually, all our entrées were on a large platter, served in the table's center. It looked like a mound of mud, surrounded by several pieces of naan.

We lunged for the bread.

The other surprise was there were no utensils. We had to eat with our hands. After a few palmfuls of ground lamb and lentils,

I caught my sister's eye. It was that look—that pre-hysteria, "I am really trying to control my face" look. My lips curled, and I was gone. I started laughing like a freakin' hyena, totally OOC. My sister did the same. Tears were running down our faces, drool from our mouths. Our father kept looking from one of us to the other, totally confused as to what was so funny. We were gasping for breath, doubled over across the table, inches from the ghoulish gruel before us. Food was flying out of our mouths as we tried to contain ourselves, to no avail.

And then the unthinkable. I fell backward off my hassock.

Well, that just sent us over the edge. Literally. Animallike noises were escaping our throats. Gales of feverish frenzy took over our bodies. Delirium set in. We had to get out of there.

Finally we did.

I regret my behavior to this day. I hope my dad didn't think we were laughing at him. I don't know what he thought; hopefully that we were just having fun in some very bizarre way. Stress can do some peculiar things to a person, and it was the last time I put myself in that position.

Once it starts, I am helpless.

Like the time a colleague and I attended the pre-funeral viewing of a coworker's spouse who had recently passed. We had arrived early and spent some time sitting outside in the car talking, waiting for some others to shield us from the awkward silence of sympathy small talk. We started laughing. And then we upped the ante. We were howling. Every time we opened the car doors we would scream with hysteria. We would compose ourselves and get to the parlor's door, then look at each other and start up again. Convulsing. Crying. Cray-cray. We almost missed the whole thing, as we were so out of control.

It was utterly inappropriate.

We laugh about it to this day, of course. Laugh is what we do. It is what it is. Not mean-spirited in the least; just a coping mechanism that, unfortunately, is very uncouth. And it's comforting to know that there are many others laughing their way through dramas and traumas, just like me.

And there's an upside.

These endorphin-enriched events are boosting my immune system, protecting my heart and burning calories. It's not all bad. American writer Madeleine L'Engle wrote, "A good laugh heals a lot of hurts." And it's true, that comical, chemical reaction reduces pain and gets you through the bad times, though totally increases the chance of really embarrassing yourself. But as a seventy-something senior, I'm not sure I really care anymore. Life is short. Being joyful in today's wonky world of anger, affliction, and anxiety is a tall order.

I'd rather die laughing.

“I wanted the world to be uncomplicated, for the good and bad to be as distinguishable as the black-and-white tiles on my floor.”

25

Black and White

Black and white.

I have been thinking about this for days now; it's something that will not leave my mind. It is haunting my waking hours, wearing on me as I sleep. Of course, it was instigated by the terrible, gut-wrenching murder of a black man, the race riots that followed, and the inequality and injustice in our wavering, weary, worried world.

Black and white.

I find it interesting that the term *black-and-white* means sharply defined, without doubt or misunderstanding. Without any gray areas. In ballet, for example, there's a right way to do things, and it's black-and-white, and it's all striving for perfection. And yet if you look at common phrases, most that have to do with white are positive, like white light, white magic, or white lie, which isn't quite so bad a lie. But the black phrases are the opposite: black magic, black market, black sheep, indicating something is not quite right; it's ominous, dark. White often represents innocence, purity, and new beginnings. Black, on the other hand, can be seen as bad or intimidating, So the idiom *black-and-white* just isn't making sense to me right now.

I keep thinking about this tenuous term and look for a point of reference in my past. And I keep hearing Michael Jackson sing that song, "Black or White." If you remember Ally McBeal, and how she couldn't shake black Barry White out of her head. That's what I've been experiencing with Michael.

And it just won't stop.

Black and white has had a far-reaching impact on my life in many, although less serious, ways. It is a color combination that has followed me, and comforted me, throughout my life. Brides wed in white. They mourn in black. And though research studies confirm that people are most attractive dressed in black, it does have a negative, although sophisticated vibe. Coco Chanel designed the little black dress, and became a household name. It became the ultimate ticket to being perceived as worldly. To me, there is nothing more chic than a black dress with a crisp white collar.

Black and white.

I purchased my first home in the early 1970s—a brick Tudor with stained-glass windows and a wraparound front porch. But most importantly, it had a bathroom with a black-and-white hexagon tiled floor. I thought it was fabulous. That house, and my feelings for it, have never left me, although today I would be hard pressed to afford it. You see, I have a Real Estate Angel. And that Angel is well versed on my need for a black-and-white tiled floor somewhere in my happy habitat. I've had entry ways, kitchens, bathrooms, studios, you name it, all deftly defined in my sophisticated signature tile.

Black and white.

Decades later, I was recruited by a design agency on Madison Avenue. My hubby was left behind to sell our house, with the black-and-white tiled kitchen floor, I will add. I was in charge of finding a home in Manhattan for us and our two dogs. Jim's bestie still lived in the city, and one night at dinner I explained to him that I was looking for a two-bedroom flat with a lovely backyard and a black-and-white tiled floor. To say his eyeballs were stuck in the back of his head is an understatement. "This is Manhattan," he said. "Impossible." Clearly, he did not understand the strength and determination of my Angel.

Days later I began my search, and after coffee on the corner, I perused the *New York Times* real estate section for our new home. Buried in the hundreds of listings was a two-bedroom flat right off Park Avenue with two fireplaces and a backyard. I made an immediate appointment and met the Realtor that afternoon. It was perfect. Two blocks from my office, soaring ceilings, huge elaborate moldings, hardwood floors—and a tiled entry and kitchen.

Black and white.

I know that these floors were made popular in the early 1900s and had a huge resurgence in the 1960s. Their simplicity makes them timeless really, like black-and-white photography. Besides, they are bold, uncomplicated, and well defined. I like that, which may be the graphic designer in me. But even more, they say "home" to me. I feel rooted, safe, familiar. But black-and-white means much more in today's world.

In 1991, Michael Jackson penned the top Billboard hit "Black or White." It stayed #1 for a total of seven weeks, having knocked off the Beatles from the record for fastest arrival on top. In this song, Jackson described his views on racism and how they have affected him and the world around him. He didn't want to be defined by his color. And he did not want the label of a different race; he wanted people to see him for his artistic abilities. His words tell us that you don't have to wait until the world magically changes; it starts with you, in your life and with the choices you make daily … choices of how to treat others, how to view others that are different from yourself.

Black or white.

But what about the gray? What about the things that just aren't clear to us, or near to us, to truly understand? Why isn't life like a chessboard, where your moves are defined and so is the outcome? I wanted the world to be uncomplicated, for the good and bad to be as distinguishable as the black-and-white tiles on my floor. How do you clarify a problem so big, so gray, so awful? A problem that makes you mad, but you don't know what to do with that anguish, anger, rage? You don't know where to move to make it better.

You listen. And then you learn.

The great thing about getting older is that you become more mellow. Things aren't as black-and-white, and you become much more tolerant. You can see the good in things much more easily rather than getting enraged as you used to do when you were young. But at the same time, you have the experience, empathy, and courage to create change. Every morning, as I sip my coffee out on my balcony overlooking a beautiful green park, I ask God to "teach us to love one another." It is my prayer for the world. And it is my daily challenge to walk the walk. The path is clear. It all starts with each of us, individually, making a change. In his song "Man in the Mirror," Jackson repeats his message by clarifying, singing, and simplifying the answer.

Look in the mirror. And make a change.

Black and white.

"Give me a man in a preppy pale blue, button-down shirt, starched and smooth, and I am weak in the knees."

26

COVID Crushing

I have a colossal crush on Dr. Fauci.

It has developed over time. These times. These tenuous, terrible, television-filled times. He's not my regular type. Those of you who know my husband, and my Wasband too, know I have always been dreamily drawn to really handsome hunks—six-footers who are smart, with a sardonic sense of humor.

Not that I haven't dated others.

I've had my share of short guys, tall guys, athletes and artists. The common denominators are that they've all been really smart, physically active, and emotionally distant; the latter being a tough, tell-tale trait from my childhood. I think this is why I am crushing on Tony. He's all three, plus a distinguished doctor. So I fully admit that I have lust in my heart.

And yes, we are on a first-name basis.

Anthony Stephen Fauci is more than happily married, as am I, which I see as a plus. You see we have a very long-distance, distant relationship. And it's complicated. It reminds me of a woman I met decades ago at a very posh Houston dinner party. She was seated on my right, and I knew she'd been married to a much older, incredibly wealthy oil man. A striking single gentleman seated across the table introduced himself and then asked her if she had a husband.

Her reply was epic. "I've had two of my own, and two that weren't."

So deterred by distance, Tony and I are limited to our FaceTime-like rendezvous in the presence of the president and the bes-carfed Dr. Brix, or when he is scheduled for a television talk show. I love that he is deftly direct, void of sensationalism, and scientifically centered. He doesn't evoke excitement or emergency, fear or foreboding, doubt or dismay. Tony tells it like it is. He directs us to follow the rules, and then we will know the outcome. He is calm and composed but bravely blunt, in his blue button-down and traditional navy suit, as he impassively informs us of the latest medical misfortunes. Give me a man in a preppy, pale blue, button-down shirt, starched and smooth, and I am weak in the knees.

Add a rep tie, and I am yours.

But Tony isn't all work and no play. Born in Brooklyn of Italian heritage, he was a budding basketball star back in his high school days on NYC's Upper East Side. After attending a private Jesuit liberal arts college, he attended med school at Cornell. He graduated first in his class. Later he would become the director of the National Institute of Allergy and Infectious Diseases, at NIH.

He has made major contributions to the understanding and treatment of AIDS. Tony has done extensive research and protocols for Ebola, SARS, and West Nile viruses and has been awarded and honored more than there is room to acknowledge. I wish I had known he was on the case when I was stepping over all those dead birds on the sidewalks of midtown Manhattan. I was afraid it was germ warfare, and I know he would understand my concern.

Tony is a smart man. And I love smart men.

I love that every briefing he attends ends on a note of encouragement but with a total lack of exaggeration. He won't make promises he cannot keep or give deadlines he cannot commit to. He gives me a sense of reality that I need right now. Things continue to be so incredibly surreal, and I look to Tony to keep me grounded—apprised but not apprehensive. He keeps my anxiety at bay, and I feel safe that he is in charge.

I recently read that he is being considered for this year's Sexiest Man Alive.

But I know celebrity won't change my Tony. He won't get the big head or abandon me for a younger, prettier model. He won't blatantly bask in the limelight as so many others do, and become conceited, cocky, or complacent. He won't hire a stylist and show up in ripped jeans and a torn, graphic tee. Tony won't start using hair gel or sporting spray tans. He won't trade in his winsome wire-rims for contact lenses or trade in the family SUV for a Lambo. No, Tony knows exactly who he is. His ego is intrinsically intact. He is the ultimate East Coast preppy.

And I am his Ali MacGraw.

So every day at five, I prepare my cocktail and wait for my date, hoping his schedule aligns with mine. If he's a no-show,

I understand. He has COVID to contain, data to dissect, calamities to conquer. He doesn't call with an apology, email an excuse, or send flowers, begging my forgiveness.

No, none of that. We are both accomplished and articulate adults, seasoned and settled. I am bright. He is brilliant. We have a decades-old understanding. No relationship is perfect. We both do the best we can. No apologies needed.

And love means never having to say you're sorry.

"No one teaches us what it's
like to be invisible."

About Face

When I looked into the mirror at sixty, I remember thinking, *Oh my, I look like my mother.* But when I looked again at seventy, I thought, *Oh my God, I look like my father.* So, for my seventy-third birthday this year, I granted myself a facelift by the gifted surgeon Dr. Melanie Petro. It was something I thought I would never do, but here I am, with icepacks strapped snugly to my cheeks, in bed and writing about it. Why? Because after two years of procrastinating and imagining how scary and painful it would be, I discovered it was a piece of cake—birthday cake, as it were. No more turkey neck, no more jowls, no more hiding behind long hair. I look like me again, and I am ecstatic.

All my friends who haven't taken the plunge are fanatically following my progress, astounded as I am. Nobody really believes there was literally no pain. But it's true. And nobody believes I don't look like the Bride of Wildenstein, or the Cat Lady of New York. It's just me—the one I remember, the one I can relate to when I catch a glimpse of myself in the mirror.

I've returned to my body.

It is uncommon for anyone to be educated on what it is like to grow old. We all seemed to enter our "Golden Years" blind as bats. We are taught on television that there are medications for our aches and pains. And lawyers that can represent us for any suspicious diseases as part of a class action suit. And alert systems for when "I've fallen and I can't get up." But nobody teaches us what it is like to be invisible, unworthy of generous glances as we walk into a restaurant or bounce down the street on a particularly promising day. No one knows, or cares, that you once had a vibrant life and a voracious appetite for adventure.

But you still do.

That is where friends and family come in … the ones who knew you when, the ones who know you best. The ones who see you as they always have. Beautiful you. But we aren't educated on how to relate to a reflection that is a stranger, the one that conjures up "Who is that person?" It is an identity crisis that we are not prepared to handle, when you feel the same inside but don't look the same outside. Nobody teaches us what's coming in our "fourth quarter." Like how to handle the loss of your parents, your spouse or friend, or, heaven forbid, your child. No one teaches you how to move from a home of thirty years to a small apartment or condominium. When everything you own has a story or a memory so poignant you don't know how to let go. Or how to savor each day as if it's your last, for it may well be.

Or you can laugh.

I have found that seeing the sardonic side of things can make all this silver-sneaker stuff somewhat hysterical. At a certain point, you don't really care what people think. You can do or be anything you want. You can dress like a gypsy if that amuses you or cover yourself in couture. What you do is nobody's business but your own. Years ago, when I moved to San Francisco, dressed to the nines in my designer "dress for success" duds, I inherited a secretary with purple hair. She was a bit older than me and way cooler. I learned a lot from her about enjoying life and just being yourself. It was a great lesson for me, always trying to be perfectly perfect.

So here I am at 73, with a rented art studio and a laptop on fire with my newfound passion of writing stories. My life is full, bursting over with creative projects and people I adore. And now, as of today, I can look into my mirror and see myself again. That girl who loves to laugh, paint, and draw, sing out loud in her car and dance around the house with abandon. The pieces match again like a finished puzzle, inside and out, and for me, it is an unimaginable high.

I'm flying.

I know some people may think that having cosmetic surgery is silly, narcissistic, and a waste of resources. Maybe so. But the way I see it, people spend their play money on things that make them feel good … plants if you're a gardener, paints if you're an artist, travel if you're an adventurer. And having elective surgery is more about looking familiar than looking younger.

And let's face it, nothing feels better than really being seen or really being heard. Aging isn't easy on anyone. A well-known social phenomenon called Invisible Woman Syndrome can make it particularly hard on women. I don't buy into the theory that if you value yourself and have stimulating interests and accomplished friends, you won't feel invisible.

But I have all that and more.

I think looking familiar is the real issue, not youth. It anchors you, lets you stand tall. It has nothing to do with age. Look at fashion icon Carmen Dell Orefice. It doesn't get any more beautiful than that. Snow-white hair and all, she's absolutely gorgeous. And so, my birthday gift to myself was a cosmetic surgeon who actually saw me. And her skill and sensitivity gifted me the ability to see myself again.

The one I knew.

In South Africa, the people greet one another on the road by saying, "Sawubona." It means, "I see you." The answer is "Here I am." In other words, you are not invisible to me. You are someone.

I like that.

My father seldom gave us advice but had a saying I remember: "It's better to be looked over than overlooked." And I think he was right. We all possess gifts of significance. Toss them into the universe like stars, and let them shoot, shine, and shimmer to sway others, inform others, invigorate others, inspire others. When you share yourself, the world becomes bigger and better and bolder. Withholding your worthiness robs the world of a grand and generous gift. And that gift is your presence.

Sawubona.

"Some things are too coincidental to be a coincidence."

28

Seven Wonders of My World

Today, I discovered that I went to junior high school, sixty years ago, mind you, with the mother of my plastic surgeon. We had moved from New York City to a tiny Mississippi town, devoid of almost anything you would desire. We only lasted a few years there, as we were all fish out of water, and it was quite the blur of my childhood. New, awkward and shy, I found it wasn't the best time of my life. But I did remember her mom. Pretty, popular, predictably predestined for a life of a Southern belle.

And so it goes.

I guess it was a coincidence that I was born on the seventh day of the seventh month at seven o'clock in 1947. I see sevens everywhere. It is without fail that I will glance at a clock wherever I am, and it will say 7:07. It is a joke with my friends. One evening I actually glanced down at my dashboard and I actually saw 7777.7 miles. I had to pull over and take a picture to have proof of my eerie experience.

You would think I would have won the lottery by now.

When I was in my twenties, I was sent to New York on a business trip and attended a cocktail soiree for a major cosmetics company as they introduced a new fragrance. As I wandered through the crowd, trying my best to look at ease, I noticed a girl across the room, fashionably dressed and faintly familiar.

I couldn't take my eyes off her.

Those of you who know me know I grew up in New York. I went to a tiny, private school with 99 students in grades 1–8. As it turned out, that slightly recognizable face was my fifth-grade friend. She finally approached me. What were the chances?

Later in my career, I had a real barn burner.

My godmother Rita was a huge influence on my life as I was growing up. I remember my mom often saying, "You should have been Rita's child." She was in retail advertising, a copywriter by trade, and as irreverent and insolent as they come. I guess that tells you what an angel of a child I was.

Anyway, Rita would tell me hilarious stories about her job and the colorful, crazy-ass people she worked with in New York and later in California. Her favorite colleague was an art director, a lovely gay man with great taste and a wicked sense of humor.

Obviously, I followed her steps careerwise. I always knew that would be my choice. As I advanced and became a supervisor, I was frequently recruited to other retailers for bigger jobs and compensation. As I started a new position in Dallas,

I wandered around my new department trying to get to know the art directors, artists, and designers. They were always a diverse group, full of mischief and fun, but enormously talented. There was one older gentleman whom everyone adored. And yes, it was him, my godmother's dearest friend from the old days in New York. We were both stunned but also delighted in our special connection. He became my guardian angel.

And so it goes.

I cannot tell you the number of times I turn on the radio and know what song will be playing. Or how many years of alike serendipitous suppers my sister and I make thousands of miles apart. Or how often I know who is calling on the phone before it is announced. It just repeats and repeats and repeats.

Some things are too coincidental to be a coincidence.

I have read that these coincidences are signs of loved ones, passed away, signaling that they are watching over us. The 7:07 definitely started after the death of my mother fifty years ago. And it is so comforting. I have also noticed that as old friends and lovers pass away, I have new coincidences. One of them is seeing 1:01 on the clock almost as often as my sign of the sevens. I have a hunch who that is watching my antics as well.

And I am grateful.

Jose Manuel Barroso wrote, "What people call serendipity sometimes is just having your eyes open." Some may think me cray-cray, and that's OK with me. I've always been a bit strange, and at seventy-three, I see no reason to change. So watch for signs. Watch for patterns. Watch for repetition. Open up to the amazing, stargazing universe in which we live. The universe is always speaking to us, sending us little messages, causing some kind of coincidence and serendipity, reminding us to stop, look around, to believe in something else, in something more and larger than ourselves.

And so it goes.

"She would wander nightly to the front porch for her little bowl of milk and nibbles, stretching lazily along the edge in ecstasy after her evening meal."

Kiki Dee

In 1974, a small orange kitten showed up on our doorstep.

We were in our first house, and the kitten seemed to complete my hilarious, hippie vision of Crosby, Stills, Nash & Young's lyrics to my very favorite 1960s song, "Our House." With lyrics that included the residence of two loving cats, the song was intensely indicative of my youthful, dreamlike state of mind. I thought my life was perfect. I had everything. A handsome husband, a spectacular job, a little brick cottage in what would become the hippest part of town.

Well, somehow the delightful dream/vision didn't turn out that way. Actually it became a nice little nightmare.

A copywriter colleague of mine at the office had purchased a small, Tudor home on Mercedes Street. It was the epitome of a 1960s boho chic cottage. Peaked roof, stained-glass windows, front porch perfect for all our macramé planters. I fell in love, and wanted one too. Amazingly, one came up for sale soon after on Monticello, a few streets over in the now, very terribly tony M Street district of Dallas. My Wasband and I went to look.

The skinned cat nailed to the bedroom wall should have been a hint.

But no. All I saw were newly stained hardwoods, fireplace flames in winter, an antique armoire, and pots of chili bubbling on the stove for all our friends. The vision was complete with a rainbow of colors flooding the rooms through those splendid stained-glass windows. Cat and all, I was sold.

We named our new little friend Kiki Dee.

She would wander nightly to the front porch for her little bowl of milk and nibbles, stretching lazily along the edge in ecstasy after her evening meal. She was timid, feral really, but slowly became less afraid of her benefactors as she grew. Eventually a larger gray cat joined her, frolicking in the grass out front. We were so notoriously naive, and were mesmerized as three tiny kittens started emerging from under the house. Rocking and rolling on the back porch as they played in the sunlight, life for them couldn't be better. Then we added an Old English sheepdog to our furry family and named him Gerald. However, he was called Gerry the Bear.

It is uncanny here, and I must digress. In college I had a bulletin board above my bed, filled with magazine swipes of fashion models and favorite clippings. Nowadays they are called vision boards. One of my clippings was an advertisement for Clubman suits. In the ad was a photograph of a handsome young mustached man walking in the rain under an umbrella with a beautiful Old English sheepdog. Daily I would cast a glance of my visual collection of hopes and dreams.

My Wasband was the spitting image of that model, and of course, Gerry completed the picture. Funny how we sometimes divine our own destiny with no actual awareness whatsoever.

I recently read that a vision board, or a dream board, is essentially a physical manifestation of your goals. It's also one of the best ways to put the Law of Attraction into practice.

A psychologist explained to me that creating a vision board is more than merely cutting out magazine pictures, putting together beautiful collages, and hoping for the best. It's a creative process, a powerful visualization tool that helps you narrow down desires through the power of choice. While you're setting clear intentions and goals, it's the Law of Attraction that magnetizes and attracts you to the opportunities you need to turn these dreams of yours into a reality.

I think it works.

But back to the cats. The next year, we built a swimming pool in our backyard as we began building a life on Monticello. Gerry the Bear grew into a monstrous-sized dog and followed my ex around every chance he got. When we separated years later, Gerry stayed with me in the house, but would not go out into the backyard, and needed to be walked every day. I couldn't figure out why, until one day I noticed four feral friends on the back porch. They hissed and shrieked when I opened the door. *Lordy*, I thought, *this is a problem*. The problem really grew when I began noticing (and sorry for the gross-out here) dead baby kittens stuck in the pool skimmers that I cleaned out weekly.

I couldn't cope with that.

And now there were eight cats lounging on the back porch sunning themselves without a care in the world. I called exterminators and anyone I could think of, but because cats were considered domesticated, nobody would help me.

Soon there were fifteen cats on the back porch, hissing and wailing and driving me insane. I couldn't go out into the backyard. They were by the pool, in the garage, under the house. It was Alfred Hitchcock on steroids.

Now you have to understand, I was in the midst of an emotional divorce and not 100 percent. To say I was immobilized with guilt and sadness was an understatement. I was an emotional wreck. Finally, I found a man who agreed that if I would purchase three large traps and a carton of canned fish fillets, he would catch the cats and take them out into the country, at a cost of hundreds upon hundreds of dollars, of course. It took over a month, but every cat was delivered to their country home, and I could finally breathe.

You just can't make this stuff up.

All because of a little, orange kitten named Kiki Dee.

"Dating in Texas as an adult was like a grim game of Go Fish. Only I was the bait."

30

The Games People Play

It didn't dawn on me until recently how playing games as children was a dress rehearsal for life. Candy Land, Careers, Chutes and Ladders—we played them all. My sister and I spent countless hours holding Parcheesi tournaments in our playroom and entertained ourselves in the back seat during our Dramamine drugged family vacations playing Crazy Eights and Old Maid. The latter being a testimonial to learning how to hide your feelings as your opponent reached slowly for that crisp card with the potato-faced woman in a pillbox hat.

I guess that was a hint that all girls should strive to get married.

On the streets of Queens, we also played "Bally." I don't know where it came from, but it now seems like something suctioned from "Lord of the Flies." We dug three holes in a row and put three sticks in each. Each player would roll a pink rubber ball across the holes, taking a stick if it stopped in one of the holes. The person with the fewest sticks unfortunately was plummeted with fastballs thrown at them at the end of the game.

I loved Clue. I loved solving the mystery of a murder, as I accurately announced, "Professor Plum with the candlestick in the library." And Monopoly, where we always tried to buy the posh properties of Boardwalk and Park Place first, thus learning a bit about money and acquiring wealth, which then became power. And that was the key to winning.

Another life lesson we learned without realizing it.

My godmother had spent years living in China, and returning to New York, she brought us many beautiful gifts. Along with sumptuous silk robes and tea sets, these included a magnificent console-sized music box and an antique ivory mah-jongg set. As all were lost in the ensuing years, I always longed for another set of mah-jongg tiles much like the ones from my childhood. My sweet husband happened upon an ad in an *Architectural Digest* for a lovely antique set that looked almost identical to the one I had described. As a surprise anniversary gift, he had it sent from New York and made our anniversary day really special. I adore it, and I now play mah-jongg on Monday nights with a lovely group of ladies in my building.

We call it The Crack Club.

In public schools, we were forced to attend gym class where young teenage girls were required to wear the most unattractive gym clothes imaginable and play team sports, something I had never done. The horror of volleyball, basketball, and softball gave me the heebie-jeebies. Being unskilled and uncoordinated didn't play well with my teen angst. I was more concerned with being hit in the head than catching or blasting a ball into or across a net—new, nerdy, and, needless to say, the poster child for Janis Ian's pensively poetic "At Seventeen."

As I grew, games turned into spin the bottle, where I experienced my first kiss. Well, kiss is an exaggeration. It took many a time in the clothes closet with some poor, pimpled, panic-stricken boy to really feel a real kiss. But at least it broke the ice. It wasn't until I went to college that my kissing skills got put to good use. It was there that our pastimes became parking out on lonely country roads in rural East Texas. What an education that was.

But I digress.

As a young married I was introduced to poker games. Not for me, but for a group of ragtag suckers lured in by my then-husband. With plenty of liquor for all the guests, the weekly bloodletting provided a good source of mad money for our household. It was also peek into a world I had yet to know. One morning I found a man asleep in my bathtub who introduced himself as "Pots & Pans." Sprinting off to the kitchen, I encountered a rather rumpled older woman making coffee who was lovingly called "Aunt Bee."

Somehow it just didn't feel like Mayberry.

Newly divorced, I was placed into games of a different kind. These games were more psychological in nature and required the strategy of chess, the determination of solitaire, and the exuberance of charades.

It was called "dating."

It seems those of us who learned early on to curb our enthusiasm provided better bait for the bachelor boys. Dating in Texas as an adult was like a grim game of Go Fish. Only I was the bait.

If I remember correctly in the 1980s, there supposedly were seven single women to one single man in the tank. The game was to hook up with someone you actually liked, but you, at that time, couldn't choose. You had to be chosen. So you found yourself at parties and those then-famous fern bars dressed to kill but not too obvious, pretty but approachable, and fun but not too animated. You could laugh, but not too loud, and drink, but not too much. The rules dictated that even though you were strategically there to meet men, you mustn't appear to care if you met anyone at all. It was exhausting.

I was terrible at it.

The results were lots of first dates that sometimes proved so boring we would turn to playing games with our suitors after drinks and dinner. One evening, on a double date with my bestie, we talked two gentleman into playing Pictionary for money. Now she and I were inseparable and were somehow telepathic that night. I would draw a tiny dot and she would guess something like "geodesic dome" and be 100 percent correct. It was truly amazing, and we netted hundreds of dollars.

The men couldn't get out of there fast enough.

Thank the Lord, many years later, I was introduced to my now husband, who is the epitome of someone who plays the cards he's been dealt with dignity, determination, and grace. Diagnosed with multiple sclerosis when we first met, he inspires many people by accepting his illness but not letting it define him. His goal is to walk again, and I have no doubt that he will do it. It may be five steps, it may be ten, but he will someday walk on his own. His sense of humor and love of people make him a magnet to those around him.

One day not long ago, one of our building residents stopped me in the lobby with his phone held out, smiling from ear to ear. "Look," he said, "it's Jim walking on the treadmill!" His unleashed joy was overwhelming.

Life doesn't always give you a great hand, but it's what you do with that hand that matters. You may not always have the best letters to put on the board in Scrabble, but you can still play a word and find some success.

So when things get tough, don't despair. Life is a game of the mind. You can either play puppet to the hands of fate or channel your mind to live your life the way you want it to be.

Me? I'll never be a puppet, so I'll take the other.

No strings attached.

"To everything there is a season."

Secrets of the Seasons

The Byrds sang that familiar lesson so well, telling us that there is a right time for everything. But what is that right time? How do we even know? What does each season mean? That is what I have been pondering for days.

When the Scottish band Marmalade hit the streets with their chart-topping song, "Reflections of My Life," I was a newly graduated young artist, whose life was taking a totally new turn. I recently heard that song on my Sirius Sixties station which got me to thinking about our lives being so simpatico with the seasons of the earth. And how each season was a visual marker of what happens to us all as we journey through life.

Spring is a marker of growth.

Obviously like the flora and fauna, we awaken, sprout, and spread our wings during spring. It is a season of vibrancy and vitality, bright colors, splendid smells, and sunshine. Spring showers nourish us, and we are full of hope, opportunity, endless possibilities. We are children, and we grow. We flourish. As children this all is true. We can be whatever we want. We soak up knowledge like sponges and are inspired, curious, insatiable. We are nurtured and safe and bask in a world of discovery, make-believe, and endless joy.

I loved that my childhood was full of imagination. I loved books and stories and painting pictures. I loved playing cowgirl and Clue. I loved making clothes, playing with my dolls, and school. Oh, how I loved school! We sang songs in the glee club and danced on Wednesdays. We had hot dog lunches on Fridays that fed our young bodies instead of our brains. I loved Latin and the little Roman courtyard I made for a school project in a cigar box, complete with a working fountain in the center. I brilliantly used one of those little rubber hand pumps to make it spurt water, right into the eye of my poor teacher when she leaned in to see my creation. I loved that I was always called on to read my essays to the class and that I was able to draw and paint when I finished my work before the rest of my schoolmates.

Then comes summer.

In the sun's razor-sharp rays, we are all about the outside. We are young marrieds, savvy singles, new executives. We are in the acquisition stage of our lives. We work hard to get ahead. We buy cars, then houses. We spend money on clothes, recognizable handbags, and beauty products. Our image comes into play, what people think, what we think of people. And the sun's bold brightness is a spotlight on us. We are the stars of our stories and the authors as well. We have beautiful children in the best of schools, designer dogs at our sides. We flash fabulous family photos, vacation in faraway places, and relish our success. Presentation is everything.

As a retail art director, I was obsessed with fashion and decor. I adored clothes. Nice clothes. And having worked in photography, my eye for detail was relentless, where every man's tie must be knotted perfectly, every line straight, every accessory right on trend, I am fastidious to this day. I walk into rooms and see lampshades askew, paintings hanging crooked on walls, pillows not perfectly plumped. It is kind of a curse as I am always arranging, rearranging. Table accessories grouped in threes. Colors aptly repeated in a room, Small patterns with large. On it goes. My husband kids me, saying, "Everything with you is a shoot." And unfortunately, he's right. But the studio lights that fill in all the cracks (and wrinkles) seem to fade, and no reflector will cushion the changes to come.

To everything there is a season.

The light softens. The sun's heat gives way to cool mornings and crisp air. Fall is coming, and we turn inward. We are warmed by autumn's colors—browns, oranges, golds. No more summer brights. We are empty nesters and turn inward. We cozy up our homes, sitting by fireplaces wondering who we are, why we are here, what our purpose may be. We search for answers and hone our belief systems. We turn to spirituality, friendships, connections. It is all about the inside now, what we think, what we feel. Are we fulfilled? Are we happy? We make changes. We change jobs, leave spouses, take the road less traveled. We make new lives for ourselves. And we feel good and content.

I think fall is my favorite season. I love the smell of burning leaves and the bright red, orange, and gold leaves on the trees in my neighborhood. I love the acorns and the squirrels scampering about hiding them for later. I used to love the chestnuts up north, their steaming scent on the streets of Manhattan. I love soft sweaters and tweed jackets and making soup and stews in my kitchen. It is a season of gleeful gatherings and wool-wrapped warmth in a crisp cashmere coverlet.

Until winter.

The last leaves fall, and the colors dissolve. The animals yawn and settle in for a deep sleep. The cool air gets colder, and the winter wind sets in. Our once chestnut hair slowly turns gray and then white, like the snow-covered lawns. We stay inside and reflect, mirroring our journey that has gone way too fast. Where did the time go? Wasn't it just yesterday? The internal thoughts that began in fall billow in our minds. We are amazed at our past, unsure of our future. But like splendid Snow Queens, we revel in what we have done, those we have loved, those we hold dear.

It is a season of gratitude and abundance. And we are forever grateful. There are holidays and homes filled with family and friends. But there is also loss. Family and friends pass away to another realm. We are the ones left. We are the ones unknowing of our fate. We fill our lives with people we adore, places we want to see, plans for the days to come. We play games and entertain our ragtag tribe of survivors.

We take care of one another, knowing we may be needing such care next.

We relish each day and know exactly who we are. We are stronger than ever as we steel ourselves against the wind and are hopeful like the children we once were. We see the world at war, polarized and poisoned. We surround ourselves with those holding the same worldview. They are our safety net, our security blankets. Together we wonder what has happened to our world.

We are in the winter of our lives, beautifully whitened like Narnia, watching the snow softly fall over the earth. It calmly covers our land with a glistening, shimmering white woolen blanket, which reflects the astounding beauty of our wondrous world and mirrors our worth. It is winter and time to forgive. It will soon be a time to sleep. And before we do, we instinctively know It is time to open our minds to other people, other views, other opinions. We must fill ourselves with acceptance and forgiveness if we are to sleep in peace. We let go of our biases and berate ourselves for our blunders. We set our record players at $33^1/_3$ while the world turns on 78. We become aware of the collective consciousness and everyone's right to think as they wish.

Our days are running out. Like Cinderella, we listen for the chimes of time that tell us that the party is over. Time to hail our last cab. Time to leave. Time to return Home.

Time to return to the plane of endless eternity when our name is called, and the ticking of our hearts ceases to sound, and time, as it is, stands still.

"I am not a daredevil, a gambler, or a foolish person. I am afraid of heights and speed. And clowns."

32

Everyday Heroes

I admit it. I am a chicken.

The anniversary of 9/11 has me thinking about courage. Last night as we lay in bed, my husband was saying how utterly courageous the men on United flight 93 were as they stormed the cockpit after their war cry of "Let's roll." He asked if I would have been part of that group. "No," I said in a somewhat small voice, "I would have been frozen in my seat."

But not him. You see, my husband is a man of courage.

I know this from one of his many incredibly sensational stories, as he has lived an unusually colorful life. But the one that comes to mind is when he was just starting out as a television art director in New York, at J. Walter Thompson. Like many young marrieds, Jim and his first wife lived in a lovely high-rise apartment in Queens. He rode the subway to and from work every day. This one evening in particular came to mind. Now whenever I have ridden the subway and metro in DC, I always made it a point to sit on a bench away from the tracks while waiting on the trains. In my mind, it wouldn't take much for a little shove to send you down into the death pit. But many people, I am amazed to report, stand toward the edge, wanting first grab at an empty seat, I assume. Not me; I will happily stand with all limbs intact.

On this particular evening, there was quite a crowd on the platform. Jim looked up from his nightly newspaper just in time to see the train's headlight in the near distance. As he looked away, he saw a gentleman fall onto the tracks. The man was struggling to get up as the train's headlight got larger and larger, closer and closer. He was on his back, and couldn't seem to leverage himself onto his feet. The train blew a whistle as it headed into the station. People were yelling at the man to get up, waving and screaming to hurry. The train was coming!

But Jim, my bravehearted husband, jumped in.

He helped the man to his feet and guided him to the cement wall. Waiting passengers helped hoist him up, and Jim, in an athlete's shape back then, jumped back onto the platform just in time as the train was braking to a stop. By then, there was a huge crowd, and the stunned man sort of disappeared into it.

Jim never saw that man again.

I asked him if he had been afraid. He told me he didn't even think, that he saw that the man needed help and he just went to his rescue without giving it another thought. He said it just seemed like the right thing to do. He was right. It is so embarrassing to tell you, I wouldn't have ever done that.

I am a big chicken.

I know that some of my panic-fueled phobias are the result of my overly cautious mother constantly telling me to be careful.

Cautious I am. I am always aware of my surroundings and take little risk. I am not a daredevil, a gambler, or a foolish person. I am afraid of heights and speed. And clowns. And a whole list of things. My mother had to stop the not-for-the-fainthearted Ferris wheel at Coney Island once because I was literally hysterical. She was afraid I was going to jump; go figure. I am not a fun date at the fair. I really don't enjoy the woods either, home of dangerous animals and ax murderers. I am at my happiest inside. "Not outdoorsy" is how my friends describe me.

But I do love change.

I love changing jobs and cities and houses. There is nothing more exciting than looking for a new home, entering strange new spaces, and seeing the endless possibilities. It excites me and gets my adrenaline going. I love making new friends, too. For someone who used to be painfully shy, I have conquered my stalled social skills. Some people hate all that. It makes them uncomfortable. But having moved many times, I am blessed with a framework of fearless and fun-loving friends all across our country.

On 9/11, I was working close to the Pentagon and saw the black-as-India-ink smoke fill the sky. We were huddled in my boss's office watching in horror as the towers fell. We knew there was a third plane headed our way. The husband of one of my colleagues was a police officer and instructed her to "get out of Arlington," as they thought United flight 93 was headed for the Capitol, a stone's throw from where we were.

My immediate boss, a brainless faux fashionista, instructed us to go back to work, shooting fashion with models from New York who were all on the verge of hysteria. This as our entire building complex had closed, and people were fleeing the area. Of course, I wanted to get home to my family, and so I announced I was leaving and anyone on my staff should do the same. It was that day that I learned I was unafraid and confident in my instincts. Coco Chanel once said, "The most courageous act is still to think for yourself. Aloud." That's what I did.

It was the right thing to do.

That's what Jim said about jumping onto the train tracks. Sometimes the only explanation is that it's the right thing to do. Knowing right from wrong is innate, but it takes courage to follow through. I am working on that courage every day. From the moment I met him, I knew I would marry him. Not just because he was handsome and smart and funny and kind. It was my instincts. I just knew.

It was the right thing to do.

"At the hands of my well-meaning mother, my head of hair would be twisted with round rubber Spoolies before the final act of fate. Then she would cut my bangs."

33

On the Fringe

"Olivia Culpo Debuts Bangs."

That was today's *New York Post's* "Page Six" headline. Ever since Louise Brooks made those fabulous flapper bangs popular in 1925, girls everywhere have been faced with the preposterous problem, "to cut or not to cut?" And I am no different. Obviously, model Olivia Culpo is no different either. Cutting that much hair is a tricky matter.

And I have had some really bad bangs.

To this day, I still have PTSD from my annual bang-cutting the night before my school picture was to be taken. At the hands of my well-meaning mother, my head of hair would be twisted with round rubber Spoolies before the final act of fate. Then she would cut my bangs. Somehow I always ended up looking like the flat-faced Mamie Eisenhower instead of the adorable Audrey Hepburn. So with my way-too-short bangs, my overly curled hair, and one of my mother's pastel cashmere sweaters, worn backward, I would slink to school to await my turn with the photographer. I can still see those snaps in my mind's eye.

Trying to look confident and cool with my pursed powder pink lips, shielding the world from my crooked and badly bucked teeth. And the photos were hideous. I dreaded hearing my father's annual reaction in his clipped British brogue: "She's making that funny face again."

Somehow my sister escaped these nightly makeovers. I guess she didn't need as much help.

As a teen, my bangs were my attempt to become an Audrey lookalike. Or at least Sandra Dee. Armed with a high ponytail and a scarf smartly stationed around my neck, I navigated my teenage angst. But when I got to college, bangs became serious business. Enter Cher and Grace Slick.

And I discovered the absolute magic of false eyelashes.

As a college freshman and a deliriously delighted sorority pledge, I learned the wonders of eye makeup from my splendidly sensual sorority sister Sue. Graced with the biggest brown eyes I had ever seen and a brain to match, she lived directly across the hall, and we became fast friends. I mimicked her ability to apply eye shadow, eyeliner, and those fabulous false eyelashes before I would ever leave my room. It was a made-to-order mask to conceal my immaturity and self-consciousness. And to top it all off, my newly enlarged, sexy eyes were enhanced with a shiny, thick, fantastic fringe of bangs. I was joyous. Cher, move over.

Then I discovered Jean Shrimpton.

Affectionately called The Shrimp, my English idol graced the cover of *Vogue* all through my college years. Dubbed The Face, she looked like an angel, fair-skinned, with long, straight brown hair, big baby blue eyes, and the most wonderful wispy bangs

I had ever seen. She was perfection personified. So naturally, my bangs were snipped to look just like hers. I dressed in scandalously short hip-hugger skirts and my poor boy ribbed knit sweaters, as I jauntily walked the campus humming songs by Gerry and the Pacemakers and The Dave Clark Five. Immersed in the British Invasion and my faux flower child culture, I painted psychedelic designs on all of my sorority house bedroom windows, declaring the Love and Peace within. I handed out flowers at the local Pizza Inn. And I dated boys from all the best fraternities. For the first time in my life I smiled in my school pictures. Not big, mind you, but I didn't look like the little scared rabbit of yesterday.

But then I graduated and entered the retail advertising world.

I inhaled fashion trends like a breath of spring air. Nothing excited me more. Off I went to work in suede hot pants and lace-up knee boots, hair hanging down my back, newly straightened at The Crimpers downtown and finished with a freshly cut fringe of thick, brown bangs that shone like glass. My wardrobe was filled with suede skirts, bright silk blouses, golden chains, and platform shoes in every color of the rainbow. I wore scarves designed by Peter Max and huge hoop earrings. I was doing great at my job. I was asked to model. I fell in love and married.

I was in heaven.

And through the years, like so many girls my age, every few years my bangs would return in their glory. Usually it would be just as I had grown them out to align with the rest of my hair. Cut, grow out; cut, grow out; cut, grow out. I have done this all my life. I don't know why I do it, but I do know that with bangs I feel more like me.

I recently cut them back once again. My best guess is that the recent resurgence of seventies fashion was a catalyst. Well, that and my sister, and friend and sorority sister Diane's insistence that I look younger with bangs. Now that I'm in my seventies, younger is a good thing. A really good thing. And maybe I am a bit cray-cray, but when I put on my Free People bell bottoms and my new platform clogs, I do feel younger.

Bangs and all.

"Superstition said one must never look into a mirror at night or by candlelight."

34

Going My Way?

It makes me wonder.

In the very early 1970s, while drinking a cup of Sunday coffee, and poring over the *Dallas Morning News*, I saw it. Every Sunday, there was a full page in the Lifestyle section of fabulous finds across the city, with a little black croquis of the to-die-for items above each description. And, there it was.

A magnificent mirrored armoire.

I had to have it. My starter husband and I had just purchased a home, and I was wild with the opportunity to decorate our new digs. The armoire was a huge sum of three hundred dollars, but the antique store owner allowed me to put it on layaway, a pay-as-you-go system that I wish existed today.

It took me about six months, but the wonderful wooden wardrobe became the focal point of our newly carpeted living room. And after years, and husbands, and a myriad of homes in cities coast to coast, it remains that still.

I love my armoire.

I grew up with antiques. It makes sense that my British father dabbled in the business, and our home was a timeless testament to Queen Anne herself. And as a young girl, I also had an English wardrobe in my room, something that descended from the original twelfth-century French armoire and now houses clothes instead of tools and arms. And of course, after I read *The Lion, the Witch and the Wardrobe* in the fourth grade, it also housed me at times, as I leaned against the back wall hoping to be transported to the magical land of Narnia.

But no matter where it was, my armoire lit up the room. There is something splendid about a freshly polished, shimmering silver mirror. It opens up a room and floods it with light. And encased in a freshly oiled, carved wooden monument, it is the perfect combination of new and old, light and dark, fashion and function. For years it held books and whatnots, overflow from the constrained closets of endless old homes. Today, after a major renovation, it contains our flat-screen television, a CD player, and stacks upon stacks of favorite CDs I have not been able to discard.

Over the years, the mirrors have begun to tarnish. But I love the way they look. Years ago, mirrors were thought to be linked to the supernatural, and people were frightened of their ability to steal a person's soul. That fear fostered the tradition of covering mirrors after a loved one's passing, so their souls would take the natural path to the Other World. Superstition said one must never look into a mirror at night or by candlelight. It was believed your own reflection in the mirror might show another figure behind. Mists and silhouettes that which are invisible to the naked eye may appear in a momentary glimpse in the mirror. After all, they have always been called a window into another world.

A spirit world.

Quite amazingly, mirrors have never frightened me. Except the one in the heart-stopping *Twilight Zone* episode "The Hitch-Hiker."

Growing up, my sister and I were freakish fans of the horror-filled television show *One Step Beyond* and Rod Serling's scary series *The Twilight Zone*. We would huddle on the couch, pillows to our fearful faces, as week after week, we were ghoulishly entertained by one eerie episode after another. Different stories horrified each of us, and now that they are being rerun on television, we continually call each other and scream, "Oh my God, the Dolls are on." That was Jamie's favorite, the little dolls that came to life and tripped and killed the young girl's mother on the stairs. My favorite, which has seriously twisted me to this day, was the terror-filled title "The Hitch-Hiker."

I can still hear his voice.

In this episode, a single woman is driving alone on a winding country road. Every so often, she notices a hitchhiker thumbing for a ride on the side of the pavement. It's always the same man. As night falls, she grows more and more frightened of him, driving faster and faster. Finally, she is forced to stop for gas at some remote rural station—you know, the ones with only two ancient pumps. As she hops back into her car, she turns the key and glances into her rearview mirror before backing up. In that mirror is the horribly haunting hitchhiker, who calmly says, "Going my way?" in a smooth, satanic voice. It seems he is Death, and she has wrecked her car hours before. He has come to escort her to The Great Beyond. He just scared the bejeezus out of me.

Now, is that a freak show?

I think of him every time I get in my car and glance into my rearview mirror. And pair that mirror with an antique armoire, and you have the catalyst for more horror-filled stories.

There is actually an award-winning short movie called *The Armoire*. You can watch it on YouTube. It is the third film in Jamie Travis's "Saddest Children in the World" trilogy following *Why the Anderson Children Didn't Come to Dinner* and *The Saddest Boy in the World*. The story line follows an eleven-year-old boy who is hypnotized to help find his missing friend. It is wonderfully weird.

Another weird wardrobe fact is that there is actually a company that sells an armoire that has a mind-blowing secret. It's advertised as "the most discreet way to grow weed" in furniture that sits boldly in your living room and produces pot plants to puff or please your friends and neighbors.

And I guess since you're growing plants, you are more of a florist than a drug dealer.

I am fascinated.

To be blatantly honest, the styling and design are questionable, and it looks more like a wooden refrigerator, which in my world would be a source of serious suspicion. But I guess in a double-wide, it may be the pièce de résistance. And I surmise that would solve the interior design decision whether to put it close to a fireplace.

However, the idea isn't lost on me. It is a great idea, just (in my opinion) poorly executed. The ultimate Green New Deal for a fast-growing millennial market. And then there are the Boomers, the ones who say they remember Woodstock. Really? The marketing opportunities for this high-end home accessory are endless.

Me? I am seventy-three years old and a product of the sixties. I have smoked my share and loved it. But now when someone says," My joints are stiff," I rarely think, *You're rolling them too tight*. However, I can honestly say I am thinking of where I might move the flat-screen and check this idea out. Think about it. Especially now that we are quarantined at home. It could change just about everything. Life could be fun again. So despite its unsightly, low-rent appearance, this armoire has high-end possibilities. And after all, we've been told, "When they go low, we should go high."

Going my way?

“On Thanksgiving, we were up with the chickens. We were up with the turkey, too.”

35

Retail Therapy

One of the hazards of working in retail are the holidays. At Christmas, although we worked in advertising, all non-selling associates were required to work on the sales floor during the lunch hour. We were assigned to the various departments, always praying for gift wrap, but no one would trust us with scissors. One year my boss and I were assigned to Men's Accessories, and we sold more eel wallets in the history of the entire company. It was the 1980s.

I was a super salesperson.

I learned this when I was in high school and went to my daddy's store one Saturday to earn some extra cash selling clothes. This was in the mid-1960s, when ladies' cotton blouses were only $2.99 and cotton skirts were $3.99. I could literally see the eye rolls of the other salesladies as I took my place on the sales floor. *The boss's daughter*, they thought; *lazy loser.*

My first customer was a quiet, genteel woman looking for a plaid blouse.

After several suggestions, I led her to the dressing room with three selections and waited as she tried them on. She loved them. I then suggested she find a few skirts that would interchange with the different mix of patterns, creating nine different outfits. She was thrilled. Then I suggested more ideas, and to make a long story short, I sold her over a hundred dollars' worth of merchandise. In those days, that amounted to about two dozen items. Everyone was stupefied, my father was delighted—and very, very proud.

The "other" salesladies treated me with a newfound respect.

I realized during the holidays, I could rake in a lot more money doing gift wrap, a service the store didn't offer. So Daddy set me up on a Formica folding table in the back of the store. I bought wrapping paper and ribbon at the dime store across the street and raided the store's window display assortment for tinsel and anything that sparkled that I could attach to the big bows I made. I had brazenly colored birds and flowers, silver stars and pom-poms, and big brass bells that tinkled at a tiny touch. I made a huge sign, taped it to the back wall, and waited.

Traffic was slow on day one, but the closer it got to Christmas, the line for gift wrap was so long I ended up handing out tickets so people could return for their gifts. The bigger the sparkle, the higher the price. Looking back, I am actually ashamed of how much I charged for the larger boxes that literally glowed in the dark. So many of the men, grasping at last-minute gifts, were three sheets to the wind when they finally got to the wrapping stage. Especially on Christmas Eve. It was an absolute madhouse. They made my day, though. I actually made thousands of dollars that week. Back then, it was a fortune.

I looked forward to the holidays every year.

Retail was in my blood, not only from my dad but from my godmother who was an advertising manager of one of the big Manhattan department stores, and later in California. I always knew I wanted to work in a store in advertising, which combined my love of fashion with my art and design education. After many mergers and acquisitions, I found myself working at a large downtown department store and also working the Thanksgiving Day Parade, which was televised on national television. This was one of the requirements of the job, as a parade is a huge undertaking, and they needed all hands on deck. Sounds like fun, right? Well, think again, because the detail and disasters involved in putting on an hour-long parade are no less than horrifying.

On Thanksgiving, we were up with the chickens. We were up with the turkey, too.

The floats started lining up at five a.m. The good news was that four hours later, everyone was in their place. The bad news was that either they were devilishly drunk or so exhausted and frozen they couldn't move. And then there were the little holiday nightmares that happened within that window. Things the public never saw, much less heard about.

I was usually put in charge of the celebrity announcers. This, I surmise, was because I had a skill at printing legibly and because I was relatively polite and patient. I would hand-print their cue cards (remember them?) and handle them during the broadcast, pacing the conversation as needed. And then I would run errands like providing hot coffee, makeup assistance, and coats and blankets. Usually, the parade hosts were very nice and well-behaved, although one year after selecting two couture cashmere coats for them to wear when the temperature began to drop, I was shocked to learn they had taken the apparel with them when they left.

Fights would break out.
Elves would get lost.
Horses would poop.
Santa Claus got plastered.
Giant balloons caught fire.
Floats broke down.
People fell and got hurt.
Santa peed his pants.

We were literally frantic for hours on end, but sometimes hysterical as well. We communicated through head sets (thank you, Madonna) and would sometimes wryly announce "Cadaver on Main and Fourth" to relieve the terrible turkey day tension. Of course there were VIPs to cater to as well: store executives, vendors, city officials. It was a circus like no other. Afterward, we all needed retail therapy, but not the kind you think. We needed a serious psyche session for our PTSD.

That would be Post Thanksgiving Stress Disorder.

Once another friend, who was actually an art director, had to quickly put on the Santa suit and greet the kiddies because the hired Santa was so drunk, he kept falling off his traditional tall throne. And at another department store, the Holiday Train, that *toot-toot-tooted* children around the vast auditorium decorated as a winter wonderland, lunged from the tracks and nose-dived into the wall. It was pandemonium.

After the parade, my dashing friend and I would head to Luby's Cafeteria, something that horrified just about everyone. We would turn down invitation upon invitation to a home-cooked turkey dinner, explaining that it was our Thanksgiving Day tradition, and we loved every minute of it. Luby's was a savory, safe, and sane change from my traditional second-family feast fiascoes. Every year, my sister and I would steel ourselves for the family secret that always reared its ugly head at those gatherings. It was always tense to say the least. I was actually grateful I didn't have to go.

But in retail, horrifying events are hardly limited to Thanksgiving and Christmas. It was a year-round plausible possibility.

Once for some reason Thomas the Talking Tree was installed in the children's department. The kids would timidly walk up to him and ask questions or touch his bark. Thomas was supposed to entertain them, give them a giggle, while their parents were busy charging up their cards on the latest children's back-to-school clothes. After several hours, the salespeople noticed the children running away from Thomas. They seemed frightened. After a quick look see by store security, it was discovered that old Thomas had a flask inside his trunk and was so snockered, he was spewing erotic expletives at the children. He was quickly escorted out of the store.

And the tree was uprooted from the children's department.

But that too was part of the fun. Retail back then was wonderfully creative and entrepreneurial. I was privileged to work with a group of guys and gals who were super smart and successful.

No idea was too crazy, no risk too great. It was The Golden Age, and we could almost do no wrong. I am so immensely thankful for that experience.

And we are still connected.

We may have lost several souls to disastrous diseases, but there are half a dozen of us who stay in touch to this day. We share memories and stories that unleash mass hysteria on a dime. There are photos that appear in our email that make us shriek with laughter, and create a flurry of texts that are beyond hysterical.

I love these guys. They are part of my history. And they are family.

I was fortunate to grow up in New York City which is just magical during the holidays. We would get up early on Thanksgiving, dressed in our snowsuits, so thick we could hardly bend our arms, and secure our spot along the parade route. I remember my excitement as the parade came down the street, the music, the floats, the sky-high balloons, and watching for Santa at the parade's end. Snow on the sidewalks, the enormous, elegant tree in Rockefeller Center, Santa Claus at Macy's, skating until our ankles ached, followed by hot cocoa at the Plaza—we did it all, every year.

It was heaven on earth.

But now on Thanksgiving, I make a cup of coffee, turn on the television, and watch the Thanksgiving Day Parade from the comfort of my couch. And I think of my colleagues. I think of the good times we had and the ones to come. Although this year things are definitely unique, I will think of them again and pray for the ones who are sick, and pray for the ones who are hurting, and pray for the ones who are fine, too. They are my abundance, and for that I am thankful.

But I am also grateful for my new friends with whom we will share this Thanksgiving holiday. It is a single twist of fate that brought us all together … to this state, this city, this building. Three couples, all in our crazy condo, will gather for a fantastic feast and celebrate not only the holiday but our close connection. It is a delightful and diverse group of accomplished and wildly entertaining friends, from all points of the compass. Everyone is contributing their favorite, familiar Thanksgiving dishes for the splendid spread. We consider ourselves very, very fortunate.

It looks like friendship. It sounds like fun.

It feels like family.

"Together we were unstoppable."

36

Soul Sisters

My big sister has ravishing red hair. I have been aware of this fact ever since I was old enough to remember all the fawning and fuss as we would walk down the street on the arms of our mom. "What beautiful red hair," people would exclaim, as my sis would toss her radiant ringlets in their direction. She would glow with glee as I stood in the background with my lips pressed tightly together.

There are countless baby photos of my sister, being the first-born and eleven months my senior. I hear this is normal as the latter babies were not so well documented. In most photos, she is smiling sweetly toward the camera as I look suspiciously sideways, always at her. There is one shot of us tap-dancing in a grade-school musical production, a Minstrel Show no less. My eyes are sharply cut to the right, and I am watching her closely for cues. She was the leader of the Petter Pack.

It was a pack of two.

As fate would have it, I ended up in her class at school, having been double promoted. And in a school of ninety-nine children, grades one through eight, the small class size was only overshadowed by the underlying competition it created. I was smart, but she was smarter. So I became clever, creative, and forged my own path, which served me well by making me daringly different from her. She was the smart one, I was the artist—one right-brained, the other left. Together we were unstoppable.

She was also my best friend.

We spent countless hours together. We played dolls endlessly, board games, cowboys and Indians. We rode our bikes all over town and roller-skated until we dropped. We took tennis lessons and ballet lessons and sewing lessons and riding lessons and were constant companions until college. When we would move to a new city, we relied on each other for everything: someone to play with, someone to talk to, a familiar face in the school cafeteria. And years later, although we shared our sorority secrets and sisters, we tended to be besties with others. We were trying out our singleness, being away from home for the first time; standing on our own two feet. Fashionably, of course, in the latest colorful Capezios and collegiate cordovan Weejuns. We dated and danced and were deliriously happy away at school. The year we graduated, she rented an apartment while I returned home.

We both needed jobs.

I was lucky, and the city transit deposited me in front of a bustling downtown department store that hired me in advertising on the spot. My sister, with a major in French, was somewhat confused as to where to apply. Asking our parents for guidance, she was told to go to an oil company, being in Texas, to get her start. With strong secretarial skills in tow and that ridiculously resplendent red hair, she rode the bus downtown and spotted the huge Mobil red horse flying atop one of Dallas's landmark buildings. With laser sharp focus, she entered the first-floor offices and applied for a job. She was hired on the spot as assistant to the office manager.

We were thrilled.

That evening proved to be a surprise as we told our parents about our exciting employment successes. When my sister asked if they had heard of EF Hutton, she learned to her surprise that she had accepted a position with a stock brokerage, not an oil company.

Oops.

But that jump started her financial career. She thrived as she eventually managed the sales assistants and helped run the office. She was Operations, Human Resources and Administration all in one. Plus she was splendid a party planning. Her boss, and future bosses, adored her (one even proposed). Years later she became a caregiver to one of her favorites as he entered the hospice stage of life. She made his favorite cookies, which his mother had made him as a child, and read him stories. They adored each other until his death.

Eventually we lived together again in that apartment, rooming with a sorority sister and our new boyfriends that we both ended up marrying. She met hers at the office; I met mine at a restaurant. Our comfy little commune, though, provided us with hilarious stories that render us hysterical to this day. We reunited with those hubbies and their eventual ever-brides for dinner one night and laughed ourselves silly.

As young marrieds, we ran in different crowds. Our lives seemed to veer from their original parallel paths. For years we saw each other on occasions but lost the BFF bond we had shared for a long time. It took the sudden death of our mom to bring us together. Suddenly we became each other's only safety net, and reality set in. We shared the shock and anguish of our lives' biggest tragedy. And like true Irish twins, we both divorced our starter husbands and concentrated on our careers. We became a family of two; the Petter Pack was back.

Divorce hardened her.

There was a period of time when my sister had a hard edge; a "get them before they get you" instinct. It kept me at a safe distance. She was irritable, insensitive, and impatient. Being the redheaded man magnet, she found herself being totally responsible for herself at a late age, and I think she was perplexed and somewhat frightened. It was the first time she had ever lived alone. But as the years passed and her self-sufficiency soared, she grew stronger and kinder, softer. Now she is one of the most caring people I know. She volunteers for many organizations and is always the first one to take a delicious dish to an ailing neighbor or friend.

Today, she is as beautiful inside as she is outside.

While as a child I was creating art projects, working on my dad's large art table as he hand-lettered signs for work, my sister spent time with our mother in the kitchen. She learned to make all our favorites and turned out to be a magnificent cook. We now share recipes and recount details of our daily lives several times a week. Invariably we cook the same daily dishes without discussing it first. We call it our Psychic Food

Network, and it creeps my husband out. We tend to buy the same clothes, although we live a thousand miles apart. We are both crafty and share techniques on our latest projects. We both love to read and share books and our latest television obsessions. We are so much alike now it is eerie. I even know it is her when the phone rings. My husband says my speech pattern changes when we talk, something of which I am totally unaware.

And we share a family history.

Not a conventional one by a long shot, but our history is filled with wonderful memories of growing up in New York and terrible tragedies as our family fell apart. We still laugh at the horrors of most holidays and family vacations, for most of which we were drugged with Dramamine in the back seat of our car. In our parents' quest to show us America's best, we were driven from the east coast to the west and another time down south. Our most vivid vacation recalls are crossing the desert at night with water bags and no air conditioning in our car. It was 115 degrees, and we were sweating like pigs. And driving for days on end eating smashed tuna sandwiches and deviled eggs from the cumbersome cooler under our feet. I can still hear my father's tone as he lost patience with my mom's absent navigation skills when he put her in charge of the map. It's amazing we ever found our way home.

From our Queens neighborhood, we drove to Mount Rushmore and Yellowstone Park, the Painted Desert and Old Faithful, to Disneyland and Knott's Berry Farm, and to St. Augustine and its world's crookedest house. We hit the highway to Niagara Falls and Montreal, saw Casa Loma and Quebec. As children we saw it all. As adults, we broadened our circle to include

Europe and the islands, and I got to the Far East. We both share a love of travel to this day.

I wish we lived closer.

As time marches on, I keep thinking it would be smart to live in the same city, "just in case." I keep trying to entice her to move my way. But after sixty years, her Texas roots are solid and her social circle full. She has countless friends and a very satisfying life, as do I. We have both settled into our retirement with vigor, talk on the phone constantly, and see each other whenever we can. I can always rely on her to tell me the truth, as I would always tell her. No pretenses or politics or people can break our bond. She is my very best friend.

Red hair and all.

“She became friendly with Dorian’s younger sisters, Georgiabell and Suzy, the latter becoming the most famous and most photographed model of her generation”

37

Lunch with Helen

I live in a foodie's paradise.

People are somewhat surprised when they hear that our sleepy Southern town is home to the country's Best Restaurant of the Year Award winner sponsored annually by the James Beard Foundation. They are always in the running, along with several other local establishments that serve up the best the South has to offer. Our menus are diverse; from traditional Alabama fare to a serious taste of Thailand, there is something special for everyone. And if you haven't had Alabama barbecue, you haven't lived.

I am in total anticipation to my upcoming ladies' luncheon at Helen, a new eatery which recently opened its doors in the very cool renovated section of downtown Birmingham. When I first saw the sign, it stopped me cold, as Helen was my mother's name. I have vivid memories of watching her prepare the most wonderful dishes, and watching her devour the singsong-voiced Julia Childs on television as she learned the art of French cooking. This was a definite departure from the traditional British fare she usually prepared, like roast lamb and beef, accompanied by Yorkshire pudding. We would breakfast on sumptuous scones with lemon curd, and sautéed kippers with perfectly prepared scrambled eggs.

We also had to occasionally endure the heinous hunk of roast cow's tongue, which literally sent shivers up my spine. My sister and I fed most of it to our gentle but gluttonous German Shepherd, who seemed to like the pimply pink provision. And the worst was yet to come. The next day, my sis and I were generously furnished with cold tongue sandwiches for lunch. Imagine unwrapping that in the school cafeteria. Eew. To this day I cannot think about it without gagging.

But then there was the heavenly orange sponge cake.

It was the best. I've been told the first recipe for it was published in London back in 1615 and passed down through generations, and obviously it was one of my father's favorites. She also excelled at various Jewish dishes, probably a product of her pharmacist dad's palate, and some Irish recipes too, as taught by her Emerald Isle mom.

Her Irish mother had a fatal heart attack years later in her Brooklyn kitchen, frying chicken livers in a solid stick of butter. I always thought that to be so strange.

Helen grew up on the Upper West Side in New York, a melting pot of immigrant families at that time. Pretty and popular, "Teetles" (as she was called) found instant prestige due to the fact her father owned a drugstore, complete with a then-very-hip soda fountain. At this after-school hangout, she and her besties organized the first Bing Crosby Fan Club, a bevy of devoted dames who swooned at the mere mention of the crooner's name. In later years, she was mad for Tom Jones, Frank Sinatra, and Harry Belafonte—and later still, for the soulful sounds of the Carpenters.

Teetles's bestie was Dorian Leigh (Parker) with whom she spent countless hours playing dress-up and trying on the latest lipsticks. They were girly girls and loved fashion and fads. She became friendly with Dorian's younger sisters, Georgiabell and Suzy, the latter becoming the most famous and most photographed model of her generation. My favorite movie, *Funny Face*, was based on Suzy's life. Dorian was wildly successful at modeling too, represented by New York empress Eileen Ford.

While my mother piddled in it all, she ultimately worked as a fashion stylist for a photographer in Greenwich Village. As a child I noticed that our mom had an elegance about her that other mothers didn't seem to possess. She was quietly dressed, and I remember her most frequently wearing pastel cashmere sweaters and woolen pencil skirts. Her earrings were always single pearls. She wore Revlon's Cherries in the Snow lipstick and Chanel No. 5. Her closet was never full, but what was there was wildly wonderful.

She loved Broadway shows and books. I know all the lyrics to *My Fair Lady* and *Gigi* and of course *The King and I*. My mother played them on our record player constantly. We saw them all on Broadway as children too, something I will always remember as magical. New York was a child's paradise for that, the museums and the magnificent library on Fifth Avenue. It was there I learned to love books. And although our mom read to us constantly, once I went solo, I couldn't get enough. Books transported me to other worlds where I met other characters who ignited my imagination.

My mom's love of books landed her a position as a book buyer for a large department store, and later, when my sister and I went off to college, she worked part-time as a sales clerk in a wonderful bookstore downtown. And she gifted me with the most unique and marvelous books, many of which I still have. Books like the lithesome love poems of Rod McKuen and Gordon Parks, and the raw realizations in the arty *The Rabbit Box* and *The Magic Box*. I still cherish the two volumes of illustrated lyrics of all of the Beatles' marvelous music and the *Griffin and Sabine* series, which sparked my passion for collage.

As lovely as she was, her eventual journey in this world took a tumultuous turn. All did not go well along the way. The glib and charming Englishman she met at the Village photography studio, and later married, had a wandering eye. There were financial problems and family tragedies. There were sorrowful secrets that hung over our home like a thick, gloomy gray fog. My mom became depressed, fragile, lonely, and lost. She died suddenly of a heart attack at the young age of fifty-four.

I wish she hadn't.

I wish my mother could see my sister and me now. She would be thrilled at how strong and secure we are. How successful we've been. She would have loved all the wonderful places in which I have lived and traveled and all they had to offer. She would adore my husband and our splendid Southern city. She would love the mountains, the parks, the flowers, and the fantastic food in our world-class restaurants. She would love that I'm going to lunch at Helen, and she would love to go there too. She would choose the warm potato soup, honey-glazed brussel sprouts and crisp roasted chicken just like me. But most of all, she would love that fifty years later, I still think of her daily with respect, affection, and gratitude. I still feel her presence around me, and I know she will be by my side as I enter the beautiful building that bears her name.

I'm not just going to lunch.

I'm going home.

“As I walked into the crimson-cloaked dining room, where she sat regally behind a large table, she quickly said to me, ‘Who is Helen?’”

38

I See Dead People

Growing up in a home laden with Ouija boards, Tarot cards, and tea leaves, it is no wonder I have always been drawn to the idea of a life form on another plane after we leave this earth. And yes, I absolutely believe in ghosts.

Because I've seen them.

If you happen to remember my mom's experience when we were in junior high school, where she woke up one night to an unfamiliar man standing by her bed and then saw his obituary photo days later in the newspaper after he had committed suicide, then you would understand. You see, the article listed his former address as our current address. He lived in this very house.

And then there was our Ouija board experience.

My mother opened the door to my bedroom as we sat stoically on the floor and asked Ouija silly teenage-girl questions like whether any breathing boy in our class fancied us. She said, "If that is real, ask what your baby sister's name was" (we were told she had died at birth, but oops, she hadn't). We asked the question and promptly watched the pointer swing swiftly spelling Helen. We looked up quickly for affirmation.

"That's silly," my mom quipped, "that's my name."

We thought nothing of it. Years later when our supposedly dead sister did actually die at forty-two, we learned of her dreadful disability and appalling abandonment, and her name.

It was Helen.

Fast-forward to high school. As I lay sleeping in my room, the first bedroom all to myself, I awoke suddenly and saw a young man, a teenager really, standing by my bed. I can see him to this day. Tallish and tanned, a loose lock of dark hair falling onto his forehead. He wore a tiny black-and-white checked shirt and wheat-colored jeans. He just stared at me, and quickly faded into a pin dot before he totally disappeared. He wasn't scary or aggressive, and I wasn't really frightened, just perplexed as to who he was and why he had come.

I wish I knew.

What I did know was when a few family members were about to pass on. In college, early one morning our telephone rang as my roommate and I dressed for our 7:30 a.m. classes. I looked at her and said, "My grandmother died." Sure enough, my paternal grandmother, whom I rarely saw or spoke with, had died from lung cancer at her home in London. Years later, as I left my mom after visiting her in the hospital, I looked down at her foot as I was leaving, and I actually thought I saw a toe tag.

I knew.

Soon after her death, I began a decade-long affair with psychics, the first of whom was a renowned woman in Dallas. She had found countless murder victims for the police department and had a stellar reputation for her accuracy and time-proven predictions. Two girlfriends and I went after work to her home for our very first readings. We were all terrified. They voted me to go in first. As I walked into the crimson-cloaked dining room, where she sat regally behind a large table, she quickly said to me, "Who is Helen?"

I was prepared. I was very, very careful when I responded, "Helen is my mother's name." Her eyes softened. "No, no, darling, your mother is in the spirit world now, and she wants you to know she is all right, and you're not to worry about her."

I don't remember much else.

I was hooked. As years passed and my quest for out-of-this-world information and guidance grew, my psychic visits became one of my passionate pastimes. Luckily, my gorgeous and gay boss (and dear friend) shared this obsession, so over the years we shared many memories of mystic visits along the way. The craziest of them took us to our appointments at a local Hilton Hotel one Sunday morning to meet up with a woman from another state who had booked us for that day.

Now to say this woman was spooky is an understatement. To say she was cray-cray is the truth. She proceeded to tell us both, in a more than theatrical tirade, that we were aliens from another planet. I couldn't get out of there fast enough. Coincidentally, a gossipy gentleman from our advertising office was at the same location catching the Cowboy Bus to the Sunday football game. He saw us together at the hotel, on a

Sunday morning no less, and reported us to personnel that very next day for having an affair.

We were in hysterics.

Soon after, our company merged with another, and we were transferred to Houston.

As we swiftly settled into our new homes, with new doctors and dentists and doggie day cares, we began to search for a new psychic. That's when we met an Irish lass with an ability to relay messages from beyond, as well as foretell the future. Like most reputable psychics (I can see you rolling your eyes), she was very religious, and felt her gift was a gift from God. Something to be shared, not exploited. Over the years, I grew very fond of her. At one of our last readings, she actually told me I was about to meet the love of my life, Jim, my now husband. Her description was uncanny, including name, children, occupation, and personal quirks that were razor-sharp recognizable. I knew the minute I met him that she was absolutely on target. She actually saw him; I am certain.

I sometimes wonder if the young man in wheat jeans standing by my bed so many years earlier was a young version of my husband. His age would be really close, and although there are no photos around our house of him in his teen years, I do think it was a possibility.

I like to think it was.

About a month ago, I had yet another ghostly glance at the other side. Again, I woke up from a distinct dream about losing my passport in Paris and saw two beings standing next to my husband, soundly sleeping on the other side of the bed. They were looking down at him wistfully. Not frightening, not oppressive. But almost adoringly. It was a man and a young boy, the former in an olive-green fishing vest and mustard-toned shirt. I remember thinking how odd it was that they were dressed like they had just been fishing. Not at all recognizable; I still wonder who they were. They never glanced my way but were totally focused on him. As with the others, they faded into the darkness.

Now I know what you must be thinking. She is certifiable if not all-out crazy. And I may be. But nobody really knows whether it is possible. We can't. We do know that, on the point of dying, most people see and speak to loved ones who have passed before them. There are pages upon pages of near-death experiences as well. And believing in ghosts hasn't stopped me from being completely content, blissfully happy, and a good person.

I love believing there is more connection after this life. My idea of heaven is where we are watching and guiding those we left behind as we return home to our loving almighty Father. It does not affect my belief in Him or my moral compass either. It just broadens my worldview, based on my experiences, knowing there is much more up there. Just look up at the vast blue sky, way up, as far as you can see. Invariably as I look up, I see a path to a wonderful new world and answers to life's mysteries. I see endless possibilities.

And I see dead people.

“I am focused. I have faith in the future and concentrated clarity on my role in it. I can see it clearly, like a freshly polished mirror reflecting a razor-sharp image.”

39

20/20

There are voices in my head.

I bet, like me, you can still hear that timed-tapping tone of Babwa WaWa's voice as she accurately announced the name of her popular television show until she retired in 2014. Known for her keen, introspective interviewing skills, the wildly popular television journalist is now in her nineties and is sinking slowly into the dreadful world of dementia. She is being shielded from any disturbing news, including the passing of her colleagues, our polarized politics, and the painful pandemic. Uncanny that the lion's share of it has been in 2020.

For me, it was a year of clarity.

The year 2020 was the most creatively productive in my life. I found peace, patience, and positivity during the world pandemic. I have improved myself both outwardly and inwardly, establishing new priorities and purpose, and accomplishing things I never thought possible. I have taken risks way outside my comfort zone and made new friends and connections from the safety of my couch. Whoever said that being quarantined would be creatively claustrophobic is very short-sighted. Just take a long look at me.

I found my purpose.

Who knew I could write stories? Not me! Being in advertising, I was quick to write compelling, quirky headlines and such, but I had always been an artist, a designer, visually trained and talented. And until I bravely attended a creative nonfiction writing class at the local university, I never thought expressing my life experiences could be so rewarding, so cathartic, so fabulously fun. Encouraged by my terrifically talented teacher, and a local Pulitzer Prize–winning journalist, I became immersed in recounting tales of my somewhat tortured and partially privileged childhood. I have literally found my voice.

I have been wildly productive.

Ever since leaving the fabulous art studio we had built onto our cozy Homewood cottage and moving to our present condo, I have been artistically incapacitated. Not this year. After an engaging appointment at a historic schoolhouse blocks from our home, I envisioned a studio, a space of my own, where I could be creative. I could paint, make jewelry, make cards, make anything I wanted. This year I did it.

Encouraged by my bestie from North Carolina, who is as fearless as they come, I signed a year's lease and made a perfect place to work. I named it Schoolhouse Art Studio and offer adult classes where you can sign up on Facebook for a menu of fun afternoons and private parties. It has been my heavenly haven this year, tons of fun, and the best decision I have ever made.

I have also learned to bake, something I have never done. And despite the caloric overload, I learned I really enjoy it. So now as we settle in nightly for our obsessive watching of *Schitt's Creek* or *Succession*, we delight in a piece of palate-pleasing pound cake or steaming scones, with our ever-tasty Earl Grey. The perfect ending to another perfect day.

I have newfound patience.

My instinct has always told me that patience was my life lesson. It's the thing I have in short supply. Having lost Jim's caregiver to COVID, then eventually another position, until recently I have filled that role. As his MS progresses, his moves are slow and shaky. It literally takes hours for him to shower and dress. He has trouble remembering things, as we all do at this stage of life, and asks a million questions a day. But I look at his handsome, kind face and always melt. He is the sweetest, most generous and funniest human alive, and I consider myself the luckiest lady in the world. I have learned this year what a privilege it is to care for him. To help him. To love him.

I am trying to make a positive impact.

Despite all the upheaval that 2020 brought to light, I have become less shortsighted about the needs of other people. Probably aroused by the news clips of thousands of cars lined up at local food banks across the country, my attention to those less fortunate has become rapt. I am attuned to the statistics of lives being lost to this dreadful pandemic. I wear my mask and wash my hands and do what we are told to do. I am doing my part. I vowed to purchase food monthly for our church's Blessings Boxes and gratefully stack cans and essentials in them. I send what I can to local charities. I fold clothes we don't wear often or need into cartons to send to those who do. I am graced with so very much, and I promised to pay forward my abundance.

I allowed myself a little nip and tuck and found the familiar me.

I know this is eye-rolling ridiculous, but looking in the mirror and not recognizing yourself is unnerving. As faces fall, there is a disconnect between how you look and how you feel. I feel thirty-five, some days maybe forty. But last year I realized my high, chiseled cheekbones could no longer handle the weight of the goose flesh hanging from them. I had looked like my mother for years, but now even she had disappeared. I was no longer a familiar face, so I fixed it. And I feel great. I know I don't look thirty-five, but I look like me, and that's all that matters. And there was no better time than during a quarantine. It's not like we were going to Nobu every night or whisking away to Monte Carlo for a long, lazy weekend.

I am back and loving it.

So what will next year bring? We don't really know. But I do know I love living my newfound life. It was good before, but it is great now. I have a viable vision and a list of new things I want to learn, places I want to see, people I want to know better than I do now. And I have no doubt I will do all these things and maybe more. I am focused. I have faith in the future and concentrated clarity on my role in it. I can see it clearly like a freshly polished mirror reflecting a razor-sharp image. And that image is me, smiling bigger and brighter than ever.

This is 20/20.

Afterword

For over three decades, I have been told I needed to write a book about my life. It seemed that what appeared to be normal memories to me, were vastly entertaining or somewhat shocking to others. And so during the 2020 quarantine, I began posting personal stories on social media, and eventually on a blog (storiesbypeggidavis.com). Amazingly, I began hearing from people all over the country asking me to write more stories. This book is the astonishing result of those marvelous messages sent to me.

Thank you so much for reading my book. I am humbled by your interest and support. If you enjoyed it, I would love for you to tell others. Your opinions are important. Send me an email or write a book review online; or do both! You know so much about me, I would love to know more about you! I can be contacted by email at

peggidavis@mac.com

About the Author

Peggi Davis was raised in New York City; earned a communication arts degree from Texas A & M University, Commerce; joined the retail advertising world as a fashion art and creative director. She was nationally recognized for creating innovative ad campaigns. Davis also served as chief communications officer for the Alabama School of Fine Arts. After retirement, she opened the Schoolhouse Art Studio. Davis and her husband live in Birmingham, Alabama.

CPSIA information can be obtained
at www.ICGtesting.com
Printed in the USA
LVHW091543270821
696281LV00006B/145